# INTEGRITY

## Starts with

## "I"

### The answer to all the world's problems

A guide on problem identification to eliminate the mistake of addressing the symptoms, never solving the problem.

> THINGS I HATE
> 1. VANDALISM
> 2. IRONY
> 3. LISTS

**The individual who sprayed this on the wall had both integrity and a sense of humor**

# Integrity Starts with "I"

Published by the Crofton Journal, Paper & Ink Co.
Produced by Brook Curtiss

ISBN 978-197-659-6735

All Rights reserved. No part of this book may be used or reproduced in any manner whatsoever without the expressed written consent of the author or his agent, except in the case of brief quotation embodied in the critical articles or review with author being credited.

Printed in the United States of America

First Edition published as:

Integrity Starts with "I"

Copyright: 2017

Cover and interior graphic design:
Kim Sawatzke, Crofton, Nebraska 68730

For more information on this title or availability of the author for public appearances, presentations or seminars,

please visit:

www.keithkube.com

The Crofton Journal
P.O. Box 339
Crofton, Nebraska 68730
www.Croftonjournal.com
Phone 402-388-4355

# Integrity Starts with "I"

## (The Answer to ALL the World's Problems)

This book will show how a lack of integrity is the single most important factor that causes all the world's problems. It will show how it prevents governments, societies, and political parties as well as businesses and individuals from being functional. The book also shows how to recognize the absence of integrity before it infects any problem solving process.

It will outline how to minimize the tendency of addressing only the symptom along with the process that must start with perfecting the definition of the actual problem. These steps are always necessary before there is any hope of actually solving any problem.

### Keith F. Kube

The same author of:

# The Grand Unification Theory of Business and Success

"Which personality trait is more desirable....... ?

Honest Conceit

or

Fake Humility "

Frank Lloyd Wright

1867-1959

# DEDICATION

## J. Paul McIntosh
Norfolk, Nebraska

December 1, 1924 - February 16, 2017

He understood and exemplified the virtue of "Integrity" better than any person I have ever known. His leadership by example (the only real way to lead) was exemplary of how to lead a very "well lived" life.

Anyone who had the great fortune to know him will agree, unequivocally, with my observations of this great man.

# DEDICATION

**Frank A. Kube**
Crofton, Nebraska

January 6, 1897 - September 17, 1973

    He was my grandfather and the man with whom I spent most of my formative years. He and my grandmother lived in the second home on the farm. That is where I spent all of my free time, with him in his workshop, when I was not doing farm work with my father.
    He was the truest example of a Renaissance Man I have ever known. He was the foundation for all of my critical thinking and the reason for my conviction to achieve and teach self sufficiency.

# Chapter Index

## The Universal Problem List

Preface ............................................................... X

1. No One Can Be Trusted Anymore ........................ 1

2. What is a Problem? .....Exactly! ........................... 19

3. World Insecurity ................................................. 33

4. A Stagnant Economy .......................................... 49

5. Inefficient Business Environment ........................ 61
   - 5.1  International Business and the Law ........... 61
   - 5.2  Corporate and Tax Law ............................. 66
   - 5.3  What Freedom and Liberty Means ............. 67
   - 5.4  Balance of Trade ...................................... 69
   - 5.5  Infrastructure .......................................... 73

6. Unemployment and the Reason for Jobs ............. 83

7. Unsustainable Welfare Systems .......................... 89

8. Health Care Costs ............................................... 95
   - 8.1  Health Insurance and Cost Containment ...... 95
   - 8.2  Antibiotics, Organic, GMOs ...................... 107
   - 8.3  Disabilities ............................................. 111
   - 8.4  Abortion ................................................. 112
   - 8.5  Addictions .............................................. 114
     - Drugs and Gambling ........................... 114
     - Pornography and Sexual ...................... 116
     - GLBTQ ................................................ 119

9. Government Dysfunctionality ............................ 123
    9.1  Problem Solving in a Democracy ................ 123
    9.2  Principles and Their Compromise ............... 128
    9.3  Political Agendas ...................................... 133
    9.4  Supreme Court and Judicial Activism ......... 137
    9.5  Tort Reform ............................................. 139

10. Bureaucracies That Never Solve Problems .......... 141
    10.1  Global Warming ..................................... 143
    10.2  EPA ...................................................... 145
    10.3  Fossil Energy ......................................... 156
    10.4  Nuclear Energy ...................................... 158
    10.5  Immigration .......................................... 159
    10.6  Education ............................................. 160

11. Dysfunctional Social Intercourse ....................... 163
    11.1  Fake News Phenomena .......................... 163
    11.2  Poverty ................................................. 173
    11.3  Crime ................................................... 175
    11.4  Prison Reform ....................................... 177
    11.5  Racism or Any Discrimination .................. 178
    11.6  Transgender Issues ............................... 181

12. Politicians Think They are Leaders? ................... 185

13. Not Knowing Your Purpose in Life ..................... 191

14. The Real Purpose for Prayer ............................. 201

Epilogue ............................................................. 207
Cover and Title ................................................... 215
Acknowledgements .............................................. 219
References ......................................................... 221
Index ................................................................. 243
Solution to All the Worlds Problems ....................... 249
The List of Universal Truth .................................... 251
Author Biography ................................................ 252

# PREFACE

It is sad it is so difficult to apply the core value "integrity" on a macro scale. It only seems possible on a micro or individualist scale because few people have a true altruistic interest for addressing the world problems. The real difficulty is there are few example of true integrity in the world with even fewer able or willing to put themselves into a position to make a difference.

To gain a position in politics with true altruism and integrity is nearly impossible because those traits practically guarantee un-electability. To learn altruism and integrity is very difficult as well with few examples from which to learn and it is certainly not taught in schools.

In an attempt to address the conundrum, I will try to show how the use of technology could provide a way for true altruism and integrity to be applied on a macro scale as it gives the ability to objectively apply "all the available knowledge" in finding a solution with the honest objectiveness necessary for achieving integrity.

An objective "computer like" analysis increases the likelihood of subsidiarity[1]: "the concept of being managed by the smallest responsible entity" to be more likely. Using this approach lets those who are most altruistic about an issue to make the decisions. This concept was nirvana and nearly impossible to even consider before the existence of the technology age of today, but it is now possible and proven by the invention of the Watson Computer[41] by IBM.

By having a way for dishonest agendas to be filtered out, the objective result should result in decisions that have integrity because they are fair, honest and sustainable, not having any possibility of distrust. Integrity is the most important ingredient in society that provides it. Integrity seems to be diminishing from the examples of chivalrousness from past generations. The value systems of the Renaissance that continued through the Revolutionary period is gradually dying. In these past times duels were fought and wars were waged when someone felt their integrity was impugned.

I will show how major problems should be defined, resulting in solutions that are quickly identified and implemented. It may not make solutions easier or less painful, but it will simplify the solution process by quickly identifying subjective bottlenecks and unnecessary obstacles. This approach is not new. It has been used for generations in most technical applications by data driven engineers and technicians. Today's problems are not any more complex, but they seem to demand quicker solutions that become very emotional and easily manipulated by slick advertising and propaganda.

Today, if a social or political problem IS ever solved or minimized, it is usually stumbled upon with the common approach of compromising some principles (things we like) while "accidentally" managing to not compromise any of our core values of Honesty, Fairness, Sustainability and Integrity.

The word "character" is often thought to describe these four core values, but it is almost always used as a "throw away" word and applied casually. This casualness diminishes the magnitude and the responsibly of someone with *real* character. The true understanding seems to be nebulous or in a diluted state by escaping the "magnifying glass" needed to detect true integrity.

The world doesn't seem to want to accept any quick solutions and no one likes to be "dictated to" or "preached at" with specific or strict instructions. Human nature seems to require a need to experience the "birthing pains" of decision making before a solution is considered, much less accepted. The "perfecting the question" approach involving integrity will not ease the "birthing process", but it will make the process more appreciated and acceptable. If this process is realized and internalized early, managers in government (politicians) will stop "kicking the can down the road". Our objective is to make our systems work and function with more permanence and less consternation. This is the logical outcome, if emotions and a lack of integrity do not interfere, resulting in making the world a better place.

It should become apparent that the peace, harmony and security we all seek is based in the fundamental concept of personal integrity. Integrity does not have any element of selfishness or individuality. The only way Integrity can exist in the world, requires all of us have it.

# CHAPTER 1

## No One Can Be Trusted Anymore
### (Real Integrity is a Verb)

It is important to realize our purpose in life is to make the world a better place. Integrity, like success, is not a destination, but a process that continues through our entire life and constantly practiced. It is lived.

It is an action, like a verb, that is constantly in motion. The word "trust" is often interchange with integrity, with the difference subtle but important. Trust is the expression observed by others with integrity the internal desire and reason we can have the ability to express it honestly.

This book is Thomistic[2] in its convictions with the idea to recast beliefs and truths as a standard process of living, managing and governing. This approach addresses the misunderstandings about what prayer is and corrects paradigms for its purpose in religion and life. An agnostic may cynically call prayer wishful thinking.

It is important to mention, I do not intend to relegate prayer to a position of lower important or as being unnecessary. Instead, it is to objectivize its function in a world where God does only logical things. There are instances in life where divine interventions seemed to happen, but the explanations for these miraculous happenings must always be rooted in logic. These happenings are logical and simply not yet understood with coincidence not proof of causation. Sometimes lightening does strike the same place twice.

Regardless if one is agnostic or believes in a God, there are fundamental core values to apply universally and consistently. The concept I propose is for the action of prayer, or wishful thinking, to be a problem solving technique and the reason we wish or pray for things in the first place.

Prayer is problem solving by a conversation with our self or our God. It is a conversation of appreciation for our talents that helps build confidence. This would be a conversation where we are thankful for our mental ability and physical gifts. We are expected to use these gifts to do his will, or by our moral compass, to make the world a better place. Like I said to my mother when I asked her: "Why do we pray?" I would remark: "We do not pray for rain, instead we pray in thanksgiving for the ability to figure out what to do it if does not rain."

This is not meant to minimize the basis of ones faith, instead it explains the fundamentals of faith as a bilateral process requiring our participation in the process where faith or personal conviction is involved. This book is not going to give the standard (sometimes insulting) pat answers or repeat the words: "world needs more prayer." This is not a debate about the power of prayer, faith and/or personal convictions. Prayer is simply a form of problem solving.

This is not a religious book nor is it designed to expound a presumptive attitude of being all knowing or omniscient. It is meant to logically connect the dots giving a better understanding of how your God works and the reason God, or the world, helps those who help themselves.

The process of perfecting the question is required in any problem solving exercise. It unifies principles consistent with the non-human, technical world. It is difficult to transfer these principles to the real "human" world because we have a "free will" but we must start somewhere. Anything worth achieving is always difficult because nothing worth having is ever free.

Today, with modern technology, we have a nearly unlimited access to do almost anything. To say this problem solving approach is not possible or impractical is not constructive. It is not acceptable to discount any attempt at perfecting the question because it is difficult. We can see the world's current problem solving method does not work very well because it is flawed with emotions and unrealistic expectations, not to mention the desire to find a solution everyone likes.

We must try to be more objective, less emotional when trying to solve the world's problems. The current approach has resulted in the dysfunctionalities of today's society. If we are not happy with the condition of today's society, something must be wrong with the approach used in addressing them.

This current system, of trial and error, did allow society to survive and arrive at this point. But with the speed of today's technology, the self correcting approach of past "slower times", no longer allows natural stopping points that limit unintended consequences. At these new higher speeds, it is difficult to notice problems before it passes the point of no return.

We must try to move and influence society by our example. In these "politically correct times" the objective is to expose dishonest agendas and stop unsustainable solutions, resulting in unintended consequences. In these times of instantaneous gratification and unsustainable short term answers, the example we set is the only way to affect this. If there is a lack of integrity, it causes the "pendulum to swing" too far, reaching disastrous positions before realizing it must be reversed.

All positions are contrasted on a spectrum that describes any condition in the world. This ensures the extremes are only a temporary part of life, by definition. We can not have "hot" with out knowing "cold" just like we can not have peace without knowing what war is. There will never be a steady state of the extremes. There can not be perfect peace or total war as the norm. There will be no "climate extremes" because nature always tries to achieve a sustainable equilibrium of mediocrity and the weather is always changing.

We must try to make the world a better place (more tolerable) a greater percentage of the time. We must also realize variations are impossible to stop because they are part of nature. "It is never what happens to us that matters, but how we deal with what happens to us."

YOU WILL BE ALL RIGHT,
JUST RUB SOME DIRT ON IT!

In a world containing over seven billion individuals there will always be problems that make life stressful. There will always be problems. They may be economic, social, political, business, family, religious, recreational, ecological, environmental or psychological with the requirement to know what it means to be ethical, laced through the list. All these functions in life cause each of us to work hard to achieve harmony with many working harder than necessary when the ethical part is ignored.

The irony that integrity is a missing element in the world and the root cause of all the world's problems is not new. Christ and other great thinkers have been teaching this message for thousands of years. If anyone can implement the answers found in this book, they would be the richest person in the world. But like eating an elephant, we can only do it one bite at a time.

The fact is the macro world is not where the solution to the problems are found. The solution is in realizing there is a lack of integrity in each one of the citizens on this planet. It is not a "light switch" that will cause the whole world to change.

It is the " I " in our own integrity that sets the example that becomes contagious, infecting the entire planet. We must all do our part in making the world a better place.

The biggest problem of making Integrity the primary driving force in society, there is no "human nature" incentive to practice it. Christ gave the world this very answer and he was crucified for bringing it up.

The answer has always existed but it has been diluted, modified, evolved and declared politically incorrect, causing it to be both misunderstood and compromised by situational ethics. It also masks the real cause of all societal problems and is exacerbated with the concept of social justice.[39]

This socialistic approach always addresses the symptoms because of a lack of integrity. The incentive to do the wrong thing is very seductive, with very few examples of real integrity shown and displayed in society. Showing integrity is not as newsworthy as a large embezzlement case. Each of us must set that example if we want to be truly successful and infect the rest of the world with the same behavior.

Most attempts at solutions are laws, that only deal with the declared symptom and outlines the penalty if someone is caught. These efforts to implement laws with penalties that only address symptoms also exacerbates the problem, benefiting the perpetrator, seldom solving the real problem.

The logic used in making these laws: "publicize the penalty to dissuade others when someone is caught" is naive and cowardly. It doesn't discourage anyone, but turns into an "arms race" to find ways to beat the system. It becomes a challenge for others to do the same thing thinking they won't be caught and the risk is worth the reward. This approach shows a lack of integrity by the application of this thinking. With our established purpose in life: "To make the world a better place than we found it and save our soul". Any other purpose is selfish and lacks integrity.

It is vital to understand the cause of any problem before it can be solved. The problem must be exactly defined before even considering any work at finding a solution along with some vision of what the solution will look like. One must exercise a logical process in problem solving. The insight of how to "perfect the question" in order to find a solution is addressed in the next chapter

When the problem is exactly defined, the solution is often simply a matter of turning the question into a statement. The implementation phase of any problem solving activity is covered in my first book and taught in most engineering logic classes. The definition of a problem is difficult because there must be integrity shown in the process of stating it in the first place.

> YOU AND GOD CERTAINLY DID A GREAT JOB ON THAT FIELD

> YEAH, YOU SHOULD HAVE SEEN IT WHEN GOD WAS RUNNING IT BY HIMSELF

The thought process of solving a problem requires knowing and understanding similar situations in the world with only similar examples of any use in the solution. The laws of physics and mathematics are constant and unwavering. Any dissimilar facts make the situation appear to be unique or sensational are useless. This "noise" or gossip is commonly known as NEWS when we see it on the major media networks. It is sad these exceptions, and not the norm, makes it interesting and distracting.

There is a considerable amount of money in spreading news (gossip) as unique, fake, different, dysfunctional, profane, despotic or horrible, because it causes curiosity.

Gossip is caused by curiosity. It is bad when it spreads lies that damages reputations. It is not gossip when the information exposes activity that is damaging to other or violates core values.

This curiosity is exploited by today's social media outlets like Facebook. Their objective is to have us become addicted and becomes a "sort of gossip" by broadcasting the information, true or not. It draws the "eye balls" advertisers need to sell their products regardless of the accuracy. The sad part is neither the information nor the products they advertise, seems constructive. They usually promote self serving or vanity products. This does little in making the world a better place with little evidence of any integrity being displayed.

If there is any good coming from this advertising, it causes a desire to acquire resources necessary so we can also acquire that product. This requires the effort called "making a living" (work) with the various ways to do that too numerable to mention.

This work activity is necessary to acquire resources to make money or acquire the resources to survive. Knowing how we truly make a living is also very helpful in understanding how the unifying "core values" can always be trusted and unwavering. It is fundamental to our being. We can only make a living by solving problems in order to help others make a living.

Of course, we should not kill or steal from other people to make our living. We should not acquire our daily sustenance through illegal or dishonest means. We must work in a fashion that is consistent and sustainable that allows the whole society to work in a similar manner. A good test is: "If everyone acted in a given way, would the result be a better, trusting world?" If the answer is "yes" we are on the right path.

These Core Values should give a fundamental foundation to how we conduct our lives. Benjamin Franklin said: "I will never compromise my "Core Values", only my principles (preferences), for the sake of harmony." What he meant: our core values of Honesty, Fairness, Sustainability and Integrity must never be violated.

## The "Core Values" are Honesty, Fairness, Integrity and Sustainability

**Honesty or Truth**: It is easily understood and makes communication efficient. It aids in fully understanding and agreeing with standard, dependable conventions in conversations that are trusted and not misleading. It allows reliable conclusions to be made and is the best known as the meeting of the minds in our society.

Truth also requires the acceptance of the laws of physics and economics. The belief in the natural conventions of math and science is: they are constant throughout the universe. Two plus two always equals four and gravity applies to all planets with mass are two examples. Propaganda is the example of the subtle violation of "truth". The example of repeatedly demanding that 2+2=6 with the hope less discerning people will eventually be believed it is a tool to steer the mass to accepting 2+2=5 as a compromise. This is why truth must be agreed to and never compromised as it can not violate another core value: sustainability. "Nothing can be hidden from eventual truth and knowledge." as quoted by David Hilbert[8].

**Fairness**: The saying, "the best law is no law", or natural law is fundamental to our psychological makeup. The second best law is a law that no one likes. This rule causes laws to be self correcting and requires everyone to give up a little of "what they like" (a principle) for the greater good. Without exception, every time I hear someone say "that is a very good law", that they love, I immediately know it is a bad law with unintended consequences that have not yet "come home to roost".

The best way to define "fair" is to test the conclusion that was arrived at democratically. If the sides were switched or the tables turned so they "had to walk in their shoes" would there still be in agreement if the "shoe was on the other foot"? Would they still accept the rule if they had to live under the same restrictions they imposed on the other side? If not, the law or rule is not fair. The Versailles Treaty[86] is an example of an unfair law.

**Sustainability or Longevity**: The laws of natural selection and evolution are examples of these words. The laws of physics or economics can not be temporarily ignored. The ability to have sustainability, if violated, always results in problems that are greater than the original problem they were trying to address.

There are numerous examples of laws that are populist and passed to keep low information voters appeased so they keep voting for them. A good example is the fuel mileage standards declared by congress. They demand that all automobiles meet a given miles per gallon number by a given date. They make this demand regardless of the limitation found by the laws of physics that show a car, weighing so much, require this many BTUs of energy to move it over a level surface on this planet.

The same unreasonable demands made of solar collectors violate all the core values. There is only so much "solar flux" available to produce energy. Collectors can not become economical if the sun doesn't shine enough. Putting nebulous standards that require collectors to make an arbitrary amount of power, regardless of the known physical limitation found by the research, voids any expectation that "law" subscribes to any of the four core values.

These are only a few examples of the lack of sustainability and integrity in the laws relating to the environment and human nature. There are numerous other examples found in various social, political or educational situations, to name a few.

**Integrity:** The misunderstanding of what is integrity, explains the reason why it is not internalized by many people in our society. The same thing goes with the word "Success". Everyone wants it but few can explain it. Both success and integrity are "tools" that must constantly be used during our life and not a destination where we arrive with either success or integrity in our pocket.

Integrity is that state of mind that perfectly mirrors and reflects our actions and speech. It is the attitude projected from firmly believing and internalizing your true inner feelings that dictates everything you do on a daily basis. It is not something one can declare, anymore than one can declare himself suave or cool. One can not declare it. If you must declare you are "suave or cool" you are definitely not those things. If you have to declare you have integrity, you do not have any.

There are several words used in political ads declaring a candidate's traits like "common sense" or "integrity". This is a very reliable clue to a fact the candidate does not fully understand either of these traits, if he must tell you he does. If someone has to declare they have integrity or common sense, the fact is they probably do not possess either trait. Integrity, like common sense, is a trait that is only assigned to you by others. It is a trait that "goes without saying". The perfect antonym (opposite) for Integrity is hypocrisy.

Hypocrisy is easiest seen and identified in others. It is criticized and impugned as a very undesirable trait. In the early 20th Century, when it is exposed and called out, it was the end of many careers in management and government. It was like the book "Scarlet Letter"[42], the syndrome with whom nobody would associate. The ability to escape the accusation of hypocrisy was considerably easier in those times. The elites and business leaders, along with the help of the media, were considerably more skilled at spinning the news with society not having time to study the validity of any story. This allowed hypocritical behavior and agendas to advance with the infection causing the birth of political correctness in the last half of the 20th century. This along with the propaganda to implement self serving agendas is the trend known today as an example of fake news.

The silver lining regarding the unchecked advancement of dishonest agendas is technology. The speed of disseminating information today is astounding. In the past, a dishonest agenda cycle was completed well beyond the point of no returned, before it was even discovered or anything could be done about it. This gave time to create bureaucracies designed to protect those agendas, usually addressing the symptom, never the problem. This led to the illogical incentives for compensation. Bureaucracies, rarely solve problems. They get more money if they don't solve them and the problem continues. If bureaucracies reduced or solve the problems, they are unfunded and the bureaucrats would lose their job.

It is not worth going to war to insist we always get every thing we like or want. The United State should not use a nuclear weapon against Russia because we lost to their basketball team. We may love our team or things like low taxes, clean environment, low unemployment, good roads, tacos or beer but don't go to war demanding we have them.

We established what "fighting words" are and what things are not worth fighting over. These items of compromise beg the question of: "how low?" or "how good?" or "how much?" for one to lower the expectations for these preference and still have it be acceptable. The amounts are only points of compromise and not worth dying for if we do not get everything we want.

Our "Principles" (things we like) are not on the list of core values of truth, fairness, sustainability or integrity. These core values are nearly absolute. Either it is, or it isn't. Either we have it or we don't. To understand the difference, from core values, is vital in learning what is negotiable and what is not. Principles (preferences) are negotiable, core values are NOT negotiable.

For example, my campaign manager is a remarkable piano player and music teacher. He said he didn't like anyone "singing off key". I said to him "that was a preference". He stopped, looked directly at me and insisted "that is a core value, something I would never compromise on!" With that said, I am sure he would not blow up the house of the student who couldn't sing.

In declaring sustainability an absolute, there is a question of how long is that period for it to be considered sustainable. In the world of animate objects and physical items made of metal, concrete, wood and plastic, engineers always analyze the durability and determine an expected life. These items wear and have a finite limit to their durability. This is where the management of these assets or ideas must be considered. Taxes are to be invested, never spent, in ways that defer or eliminate bigger expenditures in the future. This means the maintenance and upkeep of any project must be considered and budgeted for true sustainability.

In the world of laws, ideas, or formulas, these concepts must be timeless and almost perpetually sustainable. These ideas can not change with the situation nor adjusted when they become inconvenient when it is applied. This is the part of problem solving that requires a long memory and a logic string that anticipates possible unintended consequences. It also requires the seriousness of the problem to be ranked in order to determine how much time and energy can be invested in the solution. It also requires the determination of whether it is a core value or preference.

Too often the difference between Core Values and Principles, are referred to as our conscience, or something we have strong feelings about based on personal experiences in life. This can be confusing causing one to fight unnecessary emotional battles on principles that are not that important in the bigger picture. This causes a perceived uncompromising position to be wrongly considered a non-negotiable Core Value.....like my music teacher friend, with singing off key. It is not "the end of the world".  It is vital to realize the difference and knowing "which battle to pick".  Like the mantra: "Discretion is the better part of valor."

This discernment must always happen, especially in certain radical faith positions often found in cults. Some of their religious convictions are not convictions, but only principles where followers are made to think they are core values and a means to control the cult members.  When that false conviction is fully propagandized, the followers are taught they must defend it to their death.

The Middle East situation between the Arabs and Israelis, have Arab mothers hating Israel more than they love their own children. They seem to gladly bear these children only to have them die for their cause.

This is the reason why "stupid wars" start.  Followers are taught or indoctrinated that certain beliefs are true core values but, if fact, are only a preference.  This results in North Korea or the ISIS[3] situation we have today. People are killed for not accepting their declared preference of how or whom to worship or on matters as simple as how to dress.  These wars are the hardest to defend against and the most deadly, because of the lack of accepting the fundamental core values of fairness, truth, sustainability and integrity that we hold dear.

How can we defend against an enemy that wants to die for his principles and be rewarded as a martyr, more than we want to live in a country where we believe in core values?  It comes down to your convictions and whether or not to change ones beliefs because the new belief is less painful than the original.  This is the mental dynamic that must be thought through in picking your battle.

It is vital to bring forward the concept of identifying the single most important ingredient necessary for a harmonious society. This is integrity, the aspect of fully trusting the other party. All the problems we experience in the world, since the beginning of time, were caused by the absence of that single Core Value, integrity, and is the foundation for the other three Core Values.

This is why integrity is a verb that must be constantly acted out by the continual example we set. It can not be declared, but must be always demonstrated and apparent at every turn in our life and we can only hope that action is contagious after being noticed by others.

# CHAPTER 2

## What is a Problem?.....Exactly!

To make any statement that implies there is an answer to all the world's problems may sound incredible. But the exact definition of a "problem" must be perfected to accomplish this. There are degrees of everything. To what extent is "the problem" causing difficulties that impinge on individuals or society? What amount of negative impact does a problem have on life that compromises our existence, if not addressed? There will be issues that would be "nice" to address but in the greater scheme of thing, "a hang nail is not like a heart attack". One can be tolerated, while the other may kill you.

To quantify the seriousness of any problem, there are four parameters that need to be objectively defined. These are not necessarily in the order of importance as they all need to be answered if there is a hope of a solution:

1. What is the cost of the problem, in money or mortality?
2. What systemic issues are affected if not addressed?
3. What time frame is the problem impacting?
4. What is the solution going to look like?

By having answers to these questions regarding each problem, it will allow them to be quantified and ranked to see if any other problem has a higher priority and needs to be addressed first.

The part often ignored in the process of solving any problem, but very necessary to address, is to determine what the desired outcome is going to look like? This must be determined, as the solution may be more undesirable than the original problem. This must be quantified quickly to determine if the effort to solve it is worth the time and treasure. Is the solution of a high enough priority to be considered worth addressing over other problems?

*I DON'T THINK YOU SHOULD WORRY ABOUT THAT RIGHT NOW*

It is vital that the advantage or objective being pursued is stated. Is the advantage fair to the majority or cause extreme hardship for the minority? The amount of the investment that can be justified, based on the benefits derived, must also be known for any solution to become a reality and to whom the benefit will inure.

Emotions can not be eliminated, but by realizing emotions are involved and accepting the lesser of two evils, makes the answer easier to digest. There is an old Chinese saying: "The situation is impossible, but not serious." This is an example of how to remove emotion from a difficult problem solving exercises.

This approach must be objective and internalized by those working on the problem. If not, there will be less than honest or selfish agendas affecting the process. This problem solving approach is no longer taught in high school. It was superseded by "political correctness" and modernity[68]. It is missing from most college humanities curriculum, with the sciences casually addressing it in technical, non animate subjects.

Today's liberal studies seem to teach only the propaganda the professor wants regurgitated, absent of applying any logic from the objective problem solving system. There is a failure to realize the unintended consequences of their proposed solutions by not having any concept of what their solutions will look like in the limit.

Students today are taught how to work for someone else, not for themselves. They feel the short term appeasement of the community and camaraderie is more important than any result. They are indoctrinated into believing they are paid for "what they know". They do not learn "how to implement" their knowledge to solve problems that cost money and/or lives if not solved sustainably. This sort of thinking results in diplomas being closer to a "participation trophy"[49] than an accomplishment.

The current generation is simply not trained to think in logic strings with any though of what the final outcome looks like. Instead, they are indoctrinated with political correctness that requires them to be sensitive and considerate of any and all positions, regardless of its lack of relevance. This happens because they believe that political correctness is another way of describing democracy where everyone must have a say and their feelings considered, regardless of how unjustified those perceptions are.

They demand that civil discourse be adhered to because the belief that democracy works. There is a desire that everyone "feel" a part of the process, regardless of how counter-productive or self servicing. This is acceptable to the liberal cause as long as they adhere to their agenda. This lack of integrity results in the participation trophy syndrome where efforts are to be commended regardless of whether it contributes to a solution to the problem.

Nazi Germany had a similar approach to what they considered to be a fundamental problem with the used the words "final solution". Without going into the exact problem or its causing the WW II and the rise of Hitler, they were trying to address their perceived problem with a solution that lacked all the core values of fairness, truth, sustainability and most of all, integrity! This is an extraordinary example of what can happen if the fairness of the solution is ignored. The rest is history.

This does not preclude the need for a cold hearted cost analysis. The understanding of how to price any quality of life improvements must be sought and put into some measurable form, usually dollars. For example, it is not practical to eliminate the color red from society if it is a problem for very few color blind people. It is impossible to please all the people all the time. But, with the current trends in government, this could lead to entire movements where "victims" are found with bureaucracies established to help those victims who are color blind.

In Germany the victims were the German citizens. The cause of this victimization and fully propagandized, was the ignoring of the core value of fairness in the Versailles Treaty [86] that ended WW I. This was the only way the atrocities of WW II could be ignored or tolerated by the German citizens because they believed "an eye for an eye" was justified. This lack of integrity by these actions is perfectly obvious.

Most "victims" did not know they are being used or that they are victims until they are told. There are entire careers established to keep victims thinking they have a problem. The lack of integrity in this "game" is also obvious.

In the process of problem solving, it must also determine when the problem is solved. Rearranging furniture on the Titanic[6] will not have kept the ship from sinking. Bureaucracies often spend huge amounts of money on supplies, stationery and office equipment, preparing infrastructure to simply study the problem, and never really work on the actual problem.

They are only preparing to work on the symptom. Often these symptoms are nothing more than perceptions of a problem. Investing money and human resources should only be done when the four questions, listed at the start of this chapter, are answered and the problem, not the symptom, is clearly stated. It is easy to find answers if the perfectly obvious is quantified and clearly stated. Serious questions must be asked to see if there really is a problem. That process can be uncomfortable as these questions will often expose the "fly in the ointment" and expose incompetence or dishonest agendas. Often the problem is purposely avoided by focusing on the symptom. This is also popular with the "victims" as it allows them to avoid responsibility. They will probably vote for the party that sponsors that bureaucracy

When a dialogue about any problem solving methods is discussed, the first remark from someone who has been working on the problem is: "It is not that simple!" This immediately exposes their interest may not be in solving the problem and that they have a disingenuous agenda that will interfere with finding any solution. It is also a symptom of turf protection being more important than finding a solution.

Government bureaucracies are often found to "love" the process more than arriving at a solution. This mindset has recently been reversed in the election of Donald Trump with his problem solving method. Bureaucracy has little desire or incentive to actually focus on accomplishing an objective or solve any problem. This syndrome seems to be the mindset of many politicians or bureaucrats with no business experience.

> I'M SURE GLAD WE GOT IT OPEN BEFORE IT STARTED RAINING

    They have a survivalist, territorial and process mentality with a sincere belief the future or consequences of their activities will never be something with which they will need to deal. They believe they will be long gone and out of the picture when the "the chickens come home to roost". Their only objective is to survive "today" by saying, doing, spending or voting on anything that will improve their probability of surviving to the next day, week or term.

    This sense of survival is so strong, they never consider or have time to understand the long term consequences or lack of sustainability in their actions. This is a lack of true integrity that has infected the entire government with the party out of power constantly playing a game of "gotcha" in an effort to portray themselves as standing in front of a parade so they can look like a leader.

Individually, no one would honestly admit this is happening in government. But these bureaucracies, with the "whips" of these governing bodies herding congressional votes, are constantly trying to improve their survivability so they can say they are on the "winning team". This, in turn, improves their ability to "coat tail" through their next election while expending little political capital in that process of winning.

Often there are more advantages for bureaucracies to NOT solve the problem, particularly if the problem involves government bureaucracies or career individuals assigned to address an issue. Government is the only entity in the world where more money can be made if a problem is not solved.

Bureaucracies are typically awarded more funding if the problem become worse and would be eliminated if the problem is solved. There is no incentive for government to solve any problem by the way the bureaucracy is structured. Their ability to survive depends on their skill of talking about their efforts with statistics that supposedly shows improvement, but need more time and money to succeed.

The Chapter Index of this book is essentially the list of problems in the world. The logic used in making any list of problems is very important. It is important to determine if higher ranked problems were solved in some order of priority, often lower listed problems would not exist if the more important problems listed were addressed first.

Any attempt at solving a problem, out of the order of importance, will cause the syndrome where only the symptoms are addressed and not the actual problem. This "silence" about wrongly addressing symptom causes considerable difficulty when bureaucracies address only the symptoms. It requires remembering where all the "skeletons" or buried (disingenuous agendas) so those hidden agendas are not uncovered during their period of service or work.

This also explains the collusion between bureaucracies in either supporting other department's mission by providing evidence of why their work is needed or withhold information that would compromise "their turf" if exposed. This was evident in the various environmental agencies or in the case of the FBI and the CIA while addressing various security issues that resulted in 9/11. As a result of not sharing vital information about a possible attack the disaster managed to go undetected until that fateful day. If they are complicit, it also requires them to remember all the lies that are involved so it does not upset the "apple cart" if their lack of integrity was exposed.

The genius in any problem solving method is to find the similarities in the observation of that problem. In the description of the problem, there is always one ingredient missing from the list of core values. Usually, if that ingredient was added to the situation the problem would completely disappear. That missing ingredient is almost always integrity. This lacking of the ability for anyone to trust anyone else is at the heart of all the world's problems.

If universal integrity existed in the world, all the problems we have today would be solved and the world would be a much better place. If this were to happen, the only remaining purpose in life would be to "save our soul".

The word integrity is often used with few understanding the exact meaning. One of the most efficient ways to describe a complicate term is to define the antonym. The exact opposite of integrity is hypocrisy.

Integrity: The actions of anyone where their truest feelings, contained in their heart, are exemplary of their actions. If their actions are completely consistent with their deepest most private thoughts, that is integrity. The common expectation of someone is they have an honest heart and truly want to do "good" in the world.

There are those with less than pure hearts and do not act on those impure or less than honorable thoughts. This may appear to be an example of integrity but it is the struggle caused by the "human condition".

People, who always appeared to have the best of intentions, are often caught in less than honorable activity. They are caught when they are confident they won't, or hope, they won't be found out. This is hypocrisy or what a lack of integrity looks like.

In this instance I disagree with the more common definition of integrity. I feel Adolph Hitler[4] had integrity, or at least he could not be accused of hypocrisy. He hated the Jews and acted openly in murdering millions of them. He did nothing to refrain from acting on those feelings in his heart.

The state of ones heart without having the opportunity to act in a devious manner is often considered to have integrity. But, the saying "Untested virtue is of little value" also applies. Does one act exactly the same way if no one would ever find out what they are doing? If one does not hide secrets and is not afraid of anyone knowing what they do in their most private moments, they have the ultimate of integrity.

The former Democrat candidate for President, John Edwards[5], is the poster child for and a prime example of a "lack of integrity" or, if said another way, the classic hypocrite. Other very disappointing and sad examples are the Penn State head football coach Joe Paterno[13] and O.J. Simpson.[18]

The privacy expectations in society are confusing in some ways. It has evolved with the advent of political correctness. Privacy is a societal demand most have because they sense vulnerability, if too much information about their private life was known. One side of this coin is a personal security issue but the other side of the coin may be one of embarrassment if other people knew who they really are.

In the previous era of our parents and grandparents, the expectation of privacy was usually not an issue. Everyone, more or less, trusted everyone they knew with few secrets held back in the community. Small towns were notorious for this attitude. But as front porches disappeared and party lines were eliminated and television and air conditioning becoming common place, everyone seemed to "turn inward" and a Peyton Place[14] society came into being.

From my childhood days, I remember booklets were mailed annually from the county seat with the license numbers listed for every car in the county. There were telephone party lines where everyone knew everyone's business by "rubbernecking"[87]. Local newspapers told of who visited whom over the weekend and what they talked about. The fact the family was going on vacation was announced and everyone knew they were away from their home. That was probably the only time they locked their doors. There was trust in these communities, with few exceptions of dishonesty from anyone. Everyone seemed to look out for everyone else. Practically everybody went to the same church and they trusted everyone. Those of different religions were known and accepted because they all were buried by the same funeral home with the time came.

Today, with digital technology and instantaneous access to "everything", the world has changed. The attempt to protect our assets from being hacked goes without saying. But, the privacy issue has evolved to a point where privacy demands vigorous protection of their personal and less than honorable behavior. This seems to be more important than the protection of the financial assets. If these "private matters" were exposed there would probably be much embarrassment. This is another form of a "lack of integrity".

The point of describing these situations is to help identify the connection between these deficiencies in society. It ties itself to the cause of practically every problem in the world.

To demonstrate this concept, go down the prioritized list of the "problems in the world". One will realize why various problems could be eliminated if the concept of integrity was internalized and acted upon by everyone.

As one reviews the list from the chapter index, it becomes apparent the further down the list, the more those problems are only symptoms. The higher ranking problems are truly problems and most important to address. The reason to rank them is to minimizes the temptation to "dive in the middle" by trying to address a particular "pet issue" without fully understanding the "problem solving sequence", or PSS[77].

I am fairly confident of the rankings on this list. It does not minimize the personal problems we all encounter but it becomes apparent that personal problems become less important, in comparison, with the help of solutions from higher ranking problems. All the solutions require the ingredient of integrity and it is most likely the answer in most solutions, if we personally exhibit that trait in our daily lives.

This is the premise for knowing the true definition and understanding of a leader.  Leadership is lived and acted out without having to declare it.  It is the ultimate trait necessary and the aura of that trait is integrity that allows that individual to be trusted implicitly.  Jesus had the greatest integrity known to man and we still read and hear of his examples. Even though he never published a book or wrote a single word that survived, we all still try to follow his example today.

# CHAPTER 3

## World Insecurity

I believe the single more important problem in the world, not to mention for our country or individually, is providing dependable security throughout. The source of that insecurity varies but, the result is a problem caused by a lack of trust, be it individually or entire countries.

Security is also the single most difficult problem to solve and has existed since the beginning of animal life on this planet. The need to survive is fundamental and vital to procreate and feed ourselves without constantly worrying about being invaded by neighboring tribes. The irony, and it makes sense, if the problem of security is solved the other problems of the world will start to mend themselves. It can be a simple as realizing: if everyone could be trusted we would not lock our doors.

All living things develop methods and ingenious ways of trying to keep them "secure" from being eaten or destroyed. These living creatures and plants evolved and adapted techniques such as poisons, armor, camouflage, mimicry tricks, weaponry and stealth. These methods constantly evolve with an arms race mentality programmed in our DNA.

It is survival of the fittest and the foundation of the theory of evolution. Security will never be perfect or 100% reliable, but it must happen a majority of the time for society to have any hope of surviving. If it does not happen a majority of the time, we would be on the path to extinction. Nature does play the odds as well.

The need for security was the primary reason for the evolution of various forms of governments, kingdoms and monarchies with variations created and practiced over the past 10 millennia.

The kings were alpha types[19], who acquired land and wealth, and realized the need to defend those assets. He made agreements with the beta types[20], or peasants, who were resident on the land the alpha type, owned. The king wanted to protect his possession from invaders, so a system was design to sustainably provide that protection for both the peasants and his possessions.

That arrangement provided a way for supplying food for himself, his family and his servants. In return the king would provide protection to the peasants and their families by having them escape to the inside of his fortress or castle, if threatened. It soon becomes apparent, the ability to defend his people depended on an army to do the fighting and provide workers to build the fortress. These workers consisted of the young men, from the peasant stock, who needed work and were probably looking for adventure and didn't like farming, anyway.

This system was a form of a tax for lack of a better analogy and the beginning of what we know of as a bureaucracy. The king would manage the development of the infrastructure for both an army and a fortress. With the "world as his oyster" the ability to expand the kingdom was a simple as taking the adjacent land. IF he was the better organized monarchy, this usually succeeded. This evolved from the time of the Pharaohs, the Greeks, Romans, the Renaissance age, industrial age through to the present. These acquisitions of land in early time were peaceful as there was an unlimited amount of land and the inhabitants appreciated the protection. The model still survives with the only two differences being the weapons used to provide the security, and it is not peaceful today as there is no more land that is not claimed by someone else.

The extrapolation of these historic tales about these alpha males who had greater ambitions, evolved into having their defensive army serves a secondary purpose. "Offense" was now the primary reason to have an army as: "Boys will be boys and idleness is the devil's workshop." The hypocrisy is: these ambitious monarchs had no honest way of increasing their wealth other than stealing from the neighbors. If we analyze how nations were built. It was all a result of acquiring land. The saying "I took it fair and square" is a sad commentary for how civilizations evolved. The real irony is those that now have it, want the world to be peaceful and non-threatening so they do not have to work so hard to defend and/or protect it.

The lack of integrity in these past actions is not acceptable nor is it reversible. It, in no way, gives permission or justifies hostile actions against the descendants of those who did these terrible acts. They did happen and now we must try to make the world a better place by solving the list of problems I mentioned in the chapter index. The saying: "All saints have a past and all sinners have a future." is the best rationalization I can give.

The other reason why nations formed and civilized societies evolved is obvious. As the climate gradually warmed through the dark ages, less time was needed to "dig out a living". It took less time to survive. Food became easier to acquire, allowing more time to enjoy a higher standard of living. Life became easier, giving more time for art, culture, construction of cities and "thinking" to expand and enhance their life style.

This higher living standard and the cost of a standing army is expensive. Armies need to be fed and trained. It was considered a waste if they had nothing to do. If there nothing for the army to do, using it to enforce nation building was an over whelming temptation and the invasion of the neighboring kingdoms resulted. The rest is history.

It is difficult to think there will ever be a time when we can completely relax and not have something to worry about. To not be concerned about maintaining national security, may be naive and foolish, but to achieve a sustainable security, we must practice integrity if we expect others to have it, as well.

We must also realize what war is before we can know if we are truly getting closer to peace. There is also the DNA of "boys will be boys" as part of survival of the fittest, programmed into our genetics. To channel these contradicting forces for good purposes is difficult. The only way one force will overpower another is when the incentive for one is greater.

True peace is only found as our eternal reward (saving our soul) in the next life. But first, we need to experience and address this life and continually find ways to make the world a better place than we found it, for the next generation. This is true regardless if one believes in an after life. There is no other logical sustainable purpose for trying to make things better.

Survival of the fittest does not always require the use of aggression. Using a core value system requires more discipline and conditioning than that of any athlete in training. It is the training of our intellect and use of logic, by living the concept of integrity and the other core values that we must exercise to achieve this better world.

We know security threats have been constant over the entire period of human existence. They are basically physical, emotional, financial, economic, environmental and spiritual. We also know we will all die in that process called living. It will cause us all to eventually experience most, if not all, the insecurities mentioned, regardless of how hard we try to eliminate threats.

The "germ" that causes insecurity is the fear of being compromised physically or financially. It is part of life and is one of the many things with which plants and animal must deal, with the alternative being death. This problem will never go away; it can only be contained by cooperation and agreement with others on the basis of natural law.

There is no need to tell each of you to not kill or steal from anyone. It is a natural law, but there is also a natural law called the survival of the fittest. This law is the foundation for the theory of evolution. To say the full acceptance of integrity is not possible, by concluding that survival of the fittest must prevail, is not constructive. It will not be easy, but if security is to be realized there must be more incentive to have it, relative to the hypocritical saying "Do as I say and not as I do."

One may or may not believe in a God or that creationism is the only truth, but those beliefs do not help solve the world's problems. Acceptance of suffering as part of God's will violates our free will. We must try to change or stop suffering in ourselves or others, but suffering for the sake of suffering, because Christ suffered is counterproductive.

We all have talents to use and skills to apply in that effort to make the world better. The Lord or society helps those who try to help themselves and it a sin to waste the talent by simply accepting these problems as unsolvable. We all have an obligation to take action and not just "pray" that things will be better while we sit and wait for God or the Government to "do their thing". We all must do our part to help ourselves, and those we love, survive life in an easier fashion. If we do not try, it is hypocritical and violates the core value of fairness, truth, sustainability or integrity. We can not be a freeloader on society.

The acceptance of killing or stealing as being bad applies whether one is an evolutionist or a creationist. The Ten Commandments addressed this so it can apply to both belief systems, and also applies to the human race of which we are all members. The attempt to apply these commandments to both plants and other animals is a form of political correctness gone awry and not sustainable. The way natural resources are used must be factored into the core value of sustainability along with the other core values. The attempt to say the use of natural resources is a form of stealing is simply a disingenuous attempt at justifying the liberal agenda's overall goal of population control.

Security, in the human sense, means the harmonious existence of all people in the world. All cultures developed laws that helped civilizations to grow and thrive. The reason for societies to start and grow was always in an effort to make life easier. Life becomes easier with "many hands making light work" the universal reason for getting along.

Attempts at controlling the world's population are classic examples of addressing the symptom and not the problem. The problems in the world are not caused by people living to close together. If that was the problem, the world would have had no wars over the past 10,000 years. The problem is the lack of integrity between humans. The simple fact is no one can seem to have full trust in anyone.

The universal reason for laws was to temper "the survival of the fittest" mentality. Laws evolved and were designed to cause a civilization to realize the "fittest law" was not the most important or efficient law. It required the insight and reasoning so society could coexist in larger numbers and increase the likelihood of the whole species surviving. Laws gave a system to improve our ability to function as a unit or group and not as individuals. The alpha male who insists he be the only alpha male, and kills any competition, was concluded to be self defeating. It became counter productive in soliciting help for raising offspring and making a living that required finding food and shelter. This was only possible with team work.

Although prehistoric man did not specifically articulate this, they realized the natural law of things was still in effect. For prehistoric societies to survive as a community, they had "laws" that contained core values. They realized the best law in the world is no law. No one likes to be told what to do, but since the survival of the fittest is programmed into our DNA, there needs to be rules that cause the outliers to realize following the path of least resistance does not work well. Rules encouraging harmony made more sense.

They realized the result of unintended consequences if they followed the "survival of the fittest" mantra as they needed larger teams to survive. Teams do not work well if the alpha male kills all the other members of his team. This evolved into "thou shall not kill" as it was counter-productive if they follow the alpha male tendencies. Killing competitors in his small clan would compromise his ability to survive as there is safety in numbers. This can happen only if there is trust and integrity.

One does not accidentally arrive at integrity or success. They are attitudes that are learned by observing the examples of those that possess these talents. They need constant work and internalization so when there is an opportunity to apply these attributes, the talents are available to be called upon. You can not give what you do not possess. To show integrity or success, you must first possess each so you can give it to others through example.

## **Relationship between Integrity and Security**

This chapter started with the premise that security is the biggest problem on the planet and, as we have proven, the way to solve any problem is to first define it exactly. Since a perfect solution only occurs in a perfect world, these insights will show the adverse impact on society from a lack of security. But, because the world is not perfect, we can only continue to try with these insights stated here.

If security in the world was improved, the negative impact on all the other problems would also improve. The entire problem list in the chapter index is systemic and interrelated. This may not apparent at first but when a problem is fully defined the connection becomes obvious.

The fact these problems are actually symptoms of, and caused by, a lack of trust or integrity that puts these problems in a totally different light. It now becomes much easier to understand. The solution may be simply a matter of turning the exact definition of the problem into an action statement.

For example: If we address the problem of national security. The problem is not that we are concerned a foreign country invading or compromising our way of living, that is the symptom. The problem is the lack of integrity that spawns the untrustworthiness exhibited by the offending party. This lack of obvious trust automatically causes a defensive reaction. If there is little incentive for the offending party to be trustworthy, they are not likely to adopt that trait. The ways of society have programmed us into realizing it is easier and more profitable in the short term, to cheat, steal or intimidate than it is to be trusted.

The saying: "money makes the world go round" is not entirely true. The actual truth is "the lack of money makes the world go round". If every one had all the money they wanted, nobody would be doing anything. They would not work because they don't need the money. But, in a practical sense, the real truism is: "the spending of money makes the world go round". The very act of spending (or trying to spent) causes the activities for commerce that is vital in making a living for our self and our family. The energy to move about, with the gas in our cars or the food we eat and the clothes we wear while shopping, all happen before or during the process of spending. The actual spending that does eventually occur continues as we need to acquire a place to keep those items safe and available when we need them.

A side note on spending is the criticism by government economists and our parents when I was growing up, that kids are not saving enough of their money. They are too "spend thrifty" with their cash. As these kids have their own families they will need to make ends meet and their spending habits need to make a painful transition. But the irony is this group of spenders, ages 18 to 34, are vital to economic growth. If they do not spend like a drunken sailor, the economy suffers. The economy needs to have them buy new sneakers, go to movies, acquire electronic toys of all sorts and eat out with their friends. This is exactly opposite what our parents wanted us to do and contrary to what government findings thought was a problem. They were concerned so much of the population had little or not emergency savings as this was not conducive to a sustainable society.

This ironic twist takes us back to perfecting and defining the problem. In what priority should the problems of the world be addressed? All the platitudes of contrast come into play: "it is feast or famine", "one man's trash is another man's treasure", or a "penny saved is a penny earned" are all problems from someone's perspective. The most interesting contrast is in the business world, "someone's problem is always someone else's opportunity". The integrity part comes into play when honesty prevents the temptation of making problems by creating victims for opportunists to exploit.

THERE IS A LOT OF
GOOD STUFF IN HERE

DUMPSTER

Economic activity is desirable and vital with the integrity ingredient of honesty, and fairness necessary for sustainability. If we feel threatened, the natural tendency is to hunker down to minimizes any activity for fear of drawing attention to our self. There are always exceptions that will come into play with stories, even in times of war with battle in the trenches, where soldiers would deal in commerce to fill a need, even with the enemy. Regardless, the activity of working to acquire money happens, even under adverse conditions. But the lack of security under such conditions does makes life more difficult.

This economic concept is not exclusive to the United States. The whole world needs the activity of trying to spend or earn money. This must occur for economies to thrive. It is obvious that anything that promotes this activity makes things better. Anything that distracts from activity, out of fear, from perceived threats is not good.

This concept was first revealed to me in the early 1970's when I attended a lecture by Milton Friedman[53] at the University of Nebraska. His premise was: "The more businesses interact with each other, the better it is for the economy." This is obvious by its prima facie, but it leads to a false conclusion that all business interactions must be between friends or friendly parties. It is nice to do business with friends, but not necessary. After all, money is money regardless of from where it comes.

This perception is logical because all successful business transactions require trust. There are contractual agreements that are needed for a successful transaction. The trust ingredient is assumed with friends or parties known to the community. But when that familiarity or trust is missing, the transaction is less likely to be concluded, particularly if the transaction is large, occurring over time on credit. This is obviously not good and sadly, a reality in life.

The point is: trust is the missing ingredient. But a lack of trust is also only the symptom with the real problem a lack of integrity from the parties to the transaction. Both individuals must possess a degree of integrity for concept of trust to exist. This understanding must be addressed as it is in the pathway to security and necessary for the world to accomplish any commerce.

I first met Donald Trump in 2003 as a part of a consulting team. Mr. Trump is always looking for ways to improve business and he has no global limitations as to where he would not look for business transactions. If there are people anywhere who want to live better, his question would be: "What must happen for a deal to take place?"

This is the first step in the fundamental classic problem solving process. There needs to be a vision of what the solution will look like, for the process to begin.

The typical approach, for most businesses, is to look for reasons not to do business in areas where trust may be lacking. For individuals, with limited resources and being adverse to risk, the conclusion is: there are easier and safer ways to make money. The paradigm changes if we are dealing with many trillions of dollars or entire countries. The belief that trust (integrity) is required may not be absolutely true. The key to making the transaction is the initiator's reputation and his track record of unquestionable integrity.

If integrity is beyond question, it would be foolish not to do business, because of the past success and track record to that point. There is a self correcting aspect of doing business with someone with unquestionable integrity. It may be very difficult to get another opportunity because they will always have many other options from which to select.

The old adage "past performance does not guarantee future results" is still true. But with the element of integrity, if the deal "goes bad", both parties have the reputation of abiding by the rules of law under which the agreement was cast. Simply said, they will not cheat or disregard elements of the transaction that may be undesirable because they *HAVE* integrity. Once integrity is lost, it is nearly impossible to regain. If they live by the law, they will die by the law, just as in the mantra "If you live by the sword, you will die by the sword."

YOU HAVE TO TRUST ME ON THIS!

This sort of integrity is the basis for doing business with unfamiliar parties. One can not force someone to do business with you. And, you can't force someone to like you. But you can make a situation where he is unlikely to refuse the opportunity, or it would be foolish if he passed up the opportunity based upon your reputation for integrity.

The point is: the best way to keep peace and harmony with someone is to make the situation where their basic needs are best met by making a transaction with them. The best way to maintain security with another country is to begin by borrowing money from them. If they trust you to the point of loaning money because they have no data indicating anything different, they will not do anything to cause you not to pay them back.

To make this a good investment is to have your integrity prove you are "good for the money" and to have the reputation that you can be trusted. This also means the information shows the investment is good and can be trusted with the reputation of having good judgment assumed. To be completely trusted, unconditionally, is to have true integrity. That means your word is good and your past actions and your reputation shows you will pay back the money with nothing in your past indicating anything to the contrary. It also means if the unforeseen should happen, the use of laws that were designed to resolve these situations are applied fairly and honestly.

**The best way to ensure International Security for the United States from an enemy is to borrow money from those countries by selling them United States bonds.**

The best way to keep a foreign power from being a threat is to do business with them. By borrowing money from them and creating transactions with the money, a business relationship is created and that is the best insurance for preventing that country from harming us. They won't bomb their meal ticket or interfere with our cyber space because they want their money back.

If someone owes you money, you have a larger interest in their well being and success than any other individual or party. No one will do anything that would jeopardize their borrower's ability to repay your loan.

In looking over the world's horizon, it is hard to believe there are societies where money may not be their highest valued item. It is "control of that society" by those in power as the item they value most. They value control of their people more than money. This trait is the biggest problem to world peace particularly when ISIS countries demand everyone share their beliefs, leaving no option other than comply or be killed.

In some countries money is not their highest priority, as shown in the way ISIS acts and to a lesser extent North Korea. Their principles are not necessarily fueled by money. But in North Korea's case their dictator seems to be simply stupid and does not understand the difference between control and commerce. This still supports the case that integrity is vital, but if the mentality of the other party is vacuous or extremely questionable, it is like dealing with a bomb where it could explode at anytime.

Behavior like this is usually self-correcting, because it is difficult for a tyrant to maintain control over such a large population. Ideally, the technological advances of today, with the internet, will gradually expose this hypocrisy. To control the behavior of the population requires them to be undermined by keeping the people ignorant. These country's leaders behave this way because it is the only way to exert and maintain control. This is inconsistent with our value system and, as a result, they are the sources of the world's greatest security risks.

Many of these countries seem to love to hate and destroy those who disagree, more than they want money. Their objective is only in sustaining their personal hold on power and control, with no consideration for truth or fairness, much less good integrity. They may have integrity in the absolute sense, like Hitler, where the feelings in their heart are fully and openly expressed. All their actions demonstrate this, shamelessly. The only solace from this sort of scenario is, like in the case of Hitler, "Nothing can be hidden from eventual truth and knowledge."[8] This requires the prayer of St. Francis[9] to be modified: "Lord, Please give me patience and hurry up with it......"

The ultimate desire is to have sound problem solving methods, which are fair, honest, sustainable with integrity be the sole function of a true leader. Their examples must be used as a guide because they realize our individual obligation is to make the world a better place for those who follow.

# CHAPTER 4

## Stagnant Economy: Propagandized

The logic of how a lack of integrity extrapolates through society is felt by everyone, eventually. The lack of security we all sense when inevitable cycles occur is reflected in the economy and becomes contagious. Of the various types of economic models tested over the past three millennia: Socialism[76], Imperialism[74], Mercantilism[75] and Capitalism[73], the success of each model is directly tied to the degree of trust between the government and the citizens with their businesses.

The social contract of the government is to make the business environment as stable, efficient and fair as possible by having laws that reflect those core values, with tax laws that encourage the same.

The degree of trust in the government directly affects the perception of fairness thus giving security to society. This fairness directly reflects the amount of compliance the society has in following the government tax law. The more fair the government is perceived, the more willing the citizens are in following the tax and business laws it makes. It is directly tied to the integrity of all the parties involved. This ties back to the fact that government must run like a business and the object of government is to invest our tax dollars to reduce future expenses in maintaining that infrastructure.

If insecurity is felt, it is caused by a perception that options are being depleted or the feeling of being forced into picking an undesirable option. It is subjective and nearly impossible to measure, but it is evident by the domino affect it has on our society. For economies to flourish and for transactions using money to occur, integrity must be present and demonstrated along with the honest reasoning behind the various decisions investors and business people need to make everyday.

When government provisions favoring certain industries or sectors are implemented, or if "inside deals" are made to advance a particular agenda, these actions negate all principles of economics and the laws of supply and demand. There is no way to make logical sense of normal happens if these "thumbs on the scale" are sneaking into the mix of analysis. A logical outcome can not be extrapolated and the actual outcome does not make sense when it happens. Only those on "the inside" know the scheme and benefit. The outsiders can only watch helplessly.

This sort of activity demonstrates how a lack of integrity has a domino affect, causes unnecessary economic cycles to occur.

Investors realize there will be economic cycles causing stagnation in economic growth. The fact of why cycles occur is understandable and even somewhat predictable. But, if artificial influences are added, through Fed policy or special laws, the symptom of a stagnate economy is difficult, if not impossible to address. It also makes in nearly impossible to correct the result from the artificial influence causing dysfunctionality in the markets. These dysfunctions can last for years and almost impossible to reverse, bringing back a "normal economy".

The simple act of trusting the value of the country's currency is a function of integrity. The good will, faith and trust in our government are the foundation for the value we place in our money. This is integrity.

It is interesting to note, that gold as a unit of currency, requires no integrity. It is desired solely because of what it is. It is limited in quantity, not duplicable or able to be counterfeited and attractive to look at. It is considered the currency of last resort. All other forms of currency are subject to the integrity (good faith and trust) of the government whose name is on the piece of paper. Gold, instantaneously, has value the moment it is found.

*YOU WANT ME TO TRADE MY GOLD FOR THAT PILE OF PAPER? WHAT KIND OF FOOL DO YOU THINK I AM?*

There is little enough gold in the world to be rare but reasonably plentiful to be used as a unit of currency. (All the gold in the world would cover a football field about ten feet in depth.) The interesting thing about gold is, in spite of the fact it has no integrity associated with it, the metal is universally coveted by the religious, the atheists, criminals, saints, governments, the businesses or any combination of these individuals or groups. We view and use money or currency because of the integrity of a simple promise written on the bill that is made to the holder that we all believe. This contrast, when compared to currencies from other countries, is important to note and it shows a paradigm shift. The value of a country's currency is directly affected by the integrity of that country. The greater the integrity, the more valued the currency becomes.

If a governments spends money "like a drunken sailor", the good will, faith and trust in that government becomes suspect. Few would make business deals with sailors who are drunk (unless we are also drunk) or invest in a government that spends money foolishly. The same would apply to all economic transactions. IF the integrity ingredients are missing, the transaction will probably not turn out well. If the entity borrowing the money does not invest it wisely, that is not a good sign for consideration of making future loans.

The premise: the best security is to borrow money from your enemy and do business with them, still applies. Care must always be in the equation when doing business. And, like in business, good behavior and reputation count for a lot when negotiating. Trying to do business with someone who doesn't like you is similar to meeting a threatening dog. The dog will be cautious until there is an atmosphere of trust that shows you mean no harm. This may not be easy, but these are the steps necessary if we are trying to make the world a better place. Integrity is the feeling that a dog senses when it trusts you.

The integrity of our government, and the people elected to manage it, is obviously lacking based on the way the national debt continues to rise. When money is spent and not invested to control future expenses, shows a complete lack of integrity and sustainability. These situations, when spun by the media, are becoming more dishonest. These "propaganda" messages can take the same facts and make it an advantage or disadvantage, depending on which party they support.

When irresponsible actions are witnessed, this gives the impression to other borrowers they can get away with not being honest as well and it is permissible to be vacuous. If everyone around them is being irresponsible, the problem becomes contagious because they feel they can all now cheat.

Regardless, the result is the same. The decision makers do not seem to realize their actions are not consistent with being honest, fair, and sustainable and would be embarrassed if the world actually saw their true agenda in those decisions. If they have true honest integrity, we would not have the problems of unchecked spending with no way of repaying the debt. This reckless borrowing also compromises our security by diverting money to addressing symptoms and not problems.

The politicians seem to have no concept of "investing" tax dollars. Instead they "spend" tax dollars for votes. The tax dollars are supposed to be invested to minimize future expenses. "As stitch in time, saves nine" is a saying foreign to many government officials and this lack of understanding, or ignorance, directly impacts the world economy. They are spending money like a drunken sailor......and this is not met to insult sailors who drink too much.

Few laws that are passed actually address problems. Wage issues, economic, environmental and discrimination laws, to mention a few, only address the symptoms that result from a lack of integrity. All these "symptom addressing" laws have a direct negative result in the function of government, business and the economy. These laws do not stop the problem, but only address what to do with the perpetrator if caught. This leaves the lawyers who make a career arguing over the letter of the law and not the spirit of the law. The saying: "the best law is no law" is true if integrity were always present. The second best law is: "a law that no one likes." If someone loves a law, it is usually to the disadvantage of someone else. If it settles a grudge or extorts money from an advantaged group to favor a disadvantaged group, is another example of a bad law.

**The "Fairness Test" must always be applied: "If the tables were turned would they still like the law?"**

The real honesty or truth aspect of government, business and the law is subtle and difficult to discern. Fundamentally, honesty and/or truth is that statement which does not knowingly violate the laws of physics, economics or logic, to gain a self serving advantage.

The spin of propaganda, where compromise is demanded, is where dishonesty starts. If someone insists that 2+2 = 6 and you argue that it is not true, the compromise to agree on five is still dishonest and compromises integrity.

This example simplifies the insidiousness of propaganda and must be identified as soon as possible, before that propaganda infects the masses.

If something is said enough times, like in the book "1984"[10], and enough people stop questioning anything, the dishonest agenda becomes easy to implement. A lie becomes acceptable resulting in the need for large bureaucracies to keep the lie going.

There is a puzzle that appears periodically on Facebook, demonstrating how propaganda works. It lists a series of false equations leading to an unanswered equation that the reader is expected to solve. And because of the fact that 95% of all the people who tried to answer it got it wrong, I concluded this book needed to be written.

**Only for Geniuses**

if 2 = 6
3 = 12
4 = 20
5 = 30
6 = 42
then 9 = ?

The answer is to the last equation: 9 and not 90! The genius of the quiz is in understanding why it is not 90. It is elementary for most grade school math students to see the pattern. This does not require genius to solve. The true answer to the last equation is 9 = 9, and can only be 9. The "=" means "the same". For this to be a "pattern problem", it would need to say "is to" instead of "=". This pattern would result in 90 as the answer. This is how propaganda works. Giving wrong answers to previous questions will never change the fact that 9=9.

The things we learn in school and society are being forgotten or ignored and being replaced by propaganda. It is no wonder there are so many problems in the world today because people are no longer thinking but moving with the mob mentality, influenced by propaganda and making mistakes they feel the government should fix.

The function of propaganda is everywhere in our society. For propaganda to be effective, the audience must stop thinking and assume what they are told is true. There was NPR series call Car Talk[88] with "Click and Clack the Tappet Brothers" who, as MIT graduates, owned and operated a car repair shop in Boston. They were not only great mechanics, but hilarious and famous for the brilliant insights and conclusion about society. One example I remember is: **"If two people who do not know what they are talking are having a discussion, does the total amount of knowledge between the two go up or down?"**

The answer is DOWN for the following reasons: In every relationship there is a dominant or alpha personality. One of the two will be more dominant by nature. In this situation the dominant personality will convenience the recessive personality to believe worthless information.

The same thing happens in society. Much of the world's knowledge and its method of application are misunderstood, inaccurate or wrongly applied. Corner-cutting will result in less than optimal performances due to misunderstandings. Propaganda can innocently spread through wives tales causing very educated people to make wrong conclusion to simple problems. The above quiz is a classic example. The quiz is an example of how misinformation can corrupt our thinking. It is a classic example of how propaganda works, and to be a propagandist, one must compromise their integrity.

It is important to notice how very basic and fundamental logic is being ignored or forgotten. This seems to be occurring at a rate equal to the rate new knowledge is being added to the world's knowledge pool.

In 1900 Buckminster Fuller said knowledge was doubling every 100 years. Today, according to IBM, it is thought to be doubling every 24 months. With the internet and technological advances it is expected to double every 24 hours by 2025. The irony of all this new knowledge, it is being forgotten and/or misapplied at an equally fast rate. This means a major part of society will be as ignorant as people were at the time of Christ and more vulnerable than ever before, for propaganda to infect the societal thought process.

Knowledge is of little use, if the fundamentals of how to think and/or deduce are lost. No one will be able to find the correct answer to this simple quiz if left to their own devices after the infection of propaganda continually gives wrong answers.

The act of keeping the lie going becomes a daunting task as mentioned by the saying of D. Hilbert[11] "Nothing can be hidden from eventual truth and knowledge." Any lie must eventually surface as being wrong. This web of manipulation and control becomes very messy and explains why bureaucracies are difficult to eliminate. There is too much "self interest" in keeping the lie of the propaganda continuing. It is difficult to stop because dishonest money is made by those working to preserve it. This is a classic example of compromised integrity.

This infection harms business as well. Businesses that need to work with, or around, laws that violate the laws of economics are not sustainable. Their standard model of operation stops making sense and breaks down if it depends on unsustainable subsidies or outside incentives for a business to stay viable. When this occurs, the logical analysis of anything no longer applies with no possible way for investments to be strategized.

It becomes a house of cards that implodes if the lie is exposed or the subsidy is eliminated. Ideally those abused by the scheme will vote out the perpetrators of the lie. This requires integrity and those who are living by the lie are less than 50% of the population.

This explains why politicians like to spend money on keeping the propaganda spinning. This buys votes. It is sad that operating truthfully and honestly is often disadvantageous with little incentive to do the right thing.

Sadly, those who lived by rules that survived the time tested conclusions of business and physics are becoming extinct. As a result, politicians with only on their political science training, are making and implementing laws that violate our core values.

This becomes the path of least resistance and keeps the propaganda going because they have no knowledge of the other alternatives.

It should be a prerequisite that anyone running for political office should have a business background. This ensures they know the fundamental laws of business. Business experience is important. The lack of it makes about as much sense as expecting a bus driver, who has never driven a car, to safely deliver your children to school. I would never put my child on that bus, so why do we let people who never ran a business in their life, help operate the biggest business in the world, the United States Government?

The underlying theme, that is impacting all the problems we are addressing, is the lack of understanding how to operate with integrity. The scam of pretending to know or the fear of being politically incorrect by confronting this propaganda is the problem. Any attempt to deal with these issues, without the necessary skills, exhibits a lack integrity.

The problem of a stagnant or under performing economy requires us to go back to perfecting the question. What is a stagnant economy? The word "stagnant" is not an absolute term. It is a relevant term compared to past measurable economic results. The result is propaganda and largely a matter of comparison spun to advance an agenda of a minority or create a victim class of voters.

In the case of economic cycles, the problem is not the economy but the concern that those affect may not be able to sustain their standard of living. That means the nominal point must be established with the honest agenda to not interfere in a temporary attempt to improve it by using band aids. Band aids can only dress a scratch while the patient is having a heart attack.

To solve a problem and not the symptom, it is important to recognize what the solution is going to look like. In the case of the stagnant economy the solution must have the perception there are options. This gives a feeling of self reliance and fairness along with a trust the government will encourage favorable economic activities by not taxing success. This burden is particularly angering if the spending of the government looks frivolous and wasteful. This reflects back to the lack of integrity issue.

# CHAPTER 5

# Inefficient Business Environment

### 5.1 International Business and the Law

In the world of economics, the natural tendency is the always protect your own interest. The law "survival of the fittest" is engineered into our DNA. It is always present and irrefutable as well as inviolable. In a perfect world the cold science of engineering and economics gives solutions that appear cruel and heartless.

There is a natural desire to have solutions where one size fits all. When this is attempted, only the symptom is addressed and are recycled ideas of other failed attempts. Their flawed logic is to "think" their "skill", using a failed idea, will work this time with their management.

The reasoning for this approach is: addressing the symptom is the only remaining approach, that is the least painful, allowing those working on the problem to buy time waiting for other ideas to surface.

The problem that evolves with "one size fits all" approach is: integrity will usually be compromised in the attempt. There are agendas and customs along with natural tendencies that result from the "alpha male" tendencies that exists in both sexes. The individual with the greatest self interest at stake will try to take charge. Someone must be in charge, so the one who has the greatest interest and ability to get something done will try to steer the project. This situation is the norm in business and unfortunately the greatest obstacle to overcome if a solution that is fair, honest and sustainable is expected.

"Blood is thicker than water". This is where your own self interest may cloud integrity. This protectionist tendency leads to activities where they cut off their nose despite their face. This leads to many people having no noses, not something pleasant to look at not to mention the obvious idiocy.

Example of this idiocy are numerous highway and mass transit projects in the U.S. where projects were delayed or completely rerouted because of an influential person's selfish interests. The case where an individual didn't want the new transportation project to by-pass his business.

In San Francisco the BART[79] system, intended to circle the entire bay, was stopped because an owner did not want his restaurant to lose customers from the train commuters that would use BART when completed. To this day BART does not circle the bay with today's cost estimated to complete $10 Billion, compared to $100 million in 1965. The restaurant went out of business in the mid 1970's when he died. I would hate to have that legacy engraved on my tombstone.

The automobile manufactures did a similar thing in the 1930's to the city of Los Angeles. They purchased the entire mass transit infrastructure from the municipalities and dismantled it in order to force commuters to use cars instead of trains. To this day L.A. has the worst traffic congestion in the country with little in masse transit infrastructure to alleviate the problem. All this happened because of a lack of integrity from a dishonest agenda.

These examples are modest and polite in comparison to the sort of idiocy demonstrated by the ISIS movement. Their self servicing desire to use suicide bombers to advance a cause that is not sustainable, unfair and dishonest is the other extreme of the same spectrum. The only good thing about ISIS, like Hitler, is they obviously have integrity, very BAD integrity; to be so adamant in their convictions to take such extreme and corrupt measures that violate all the other core values or any sense of human dignity and decency.

But ISIS and Hitler did it openly and there is no doubt about the emotional or ambivalent state of their hearts. I grant that Hitler was brilliant in disguising his hypocrisy to the German citizens, but the convictions of his position regarding the Jewish population was fairly evident to those outside the propaganda that covered Germany.

The hypocrisy of the restaurant owner or the car companies is not as easily detected, but another example of how unintended consequences, from a lack of integrity can leave lasting scares regardless of how blatant or subtle the hypocrisy. With the core values of honesty, fairness, sustainability and integrity all actions, laws, agreements and understandings will naturally have these values as a foundation.

Benjamin Franklin[21] said: "I will never compromise my Core Values, but I will consider giving up things I prefer, to reach an agreement"

This means there are things we all prefer, like lower taxes, clean environment, low unemployment, privacy or education. These values are not core and must be understood as negotiable preferences that are more or less desirable. Which preference is most important and to what degree are we willing to compromise on these preferences is the question. Most would agree that lower taxes, with a clean environment, with everyone working after getting a good education are good things. But in life there is no such thing as nirvana or perfection. Which preferences are we willing to compromise and which preference is a higher priority? The irony is there is no difference between the two political parties in this country; it is simply the difference in the order of their preferences.

The aspect of what it means to compromise must be addressed. The misunderstanding of what is a preference and comparing it to core values is negotiating a lie. To compromise on a core value means that you are expected to agree that 2+2= 6 and then eventually agree that 2+2=5. This misperception that everything is negotiable is false and very dangerous, if that is what is expected. This sort of compromise has evolved into political correctness. It is a result of a false paradigm where it is not nice to correct an obvious fallacy. Political correctness also leads to having it be acceptable to criticize someone for being closed minded, racist or bigoted if they do not consider "5" as an acceptable answer, but unacceptable to criticize them if one disagrees with liberal agendas. In short, political correctness means always agreeing with the liberal point of view.

In further analysis, the actual cause of any war is very simple and infallible. It is not possible to disagree with any of the core values of Fairness, Honesty, Integrity or Sustainability. Our common goal is a peaceful, harmonious world. We all have preferences and bias. No one should be expected to compromise a core value in a way of getting along. That is hypocrisy. The compromise can only be on preference items or on things we would like, but could live without.

In a situation where a society is expected compromise on a core value is the cause for all wars. All wars in the history were started because of this violation. A demand or expectation to compromise on any of these core values: truth, fairness, integrity or sustainability are fighting words and the only reason for ever starting a war.

In contrast, there are hurt feelings and some angst when preferences are compromised, but it is not worth going to war when resisting compromise on preference items.

Again, the lack of integrity continues to be laced through all the situations regarding all laws from common to International law and other legal situations. It is as simple as having the trust in the entities doing the negotiations. If there is unwavering trust and assurances there will be no cheating at any point, the problem is solved. The concept of fairness means the situation would still be acceptable if the tables were turned.

The Trans-Pacific Trade agreement is a very good law and would work perfectly if there is trust (Integrity) in all the aspects of implementation. When trust and integrity happens "the spirit of the law" will prevail. If there is no trust, only the symptom of the problem will be addressed with tariffs and taxes. This is in an effort to cause the pain for cheating that is greater than the pain of non-compliance. Again, the lack of integrity is the cause of the problem. The treaties are only efforts to address the symptom if anyone is caught cheating.

The integrity of each country is what gets the parties to the table. It is the strength of that integrity that allows the agreement to be forged along with the reputation to follow through. If the president of a country is known to be weak, naive, incompetent or very non-confrontational, the chances of having an agreement make any real difference is small. History if filled with examples where these "games of chicken" occurred with disastrous results. Hitler played Britain like a fiddle, when Neville Chamberlain[50] was negotiating with Hitler before WW II started.

### 5.2 Corporate Tax Law

The same principles apply as outlined above, to our corporate environment and tax laws in the United States. These examples are not exclusive to this country but prevalent universally.

The function of tax law should always be used as a way to encourage favorable business activity. The foundation of how the tax law should be used is: for funding investments in infrastructure and management that result in deferring future expenses. Taxes should never be spent. Like all business transactions, the use of money is only for investment. In the business world there is a profit motive for the investors. If there was no profit motive, the ability to attract money is missing and the likely hood of being able to expand or grow sustainably is greatly reduced if not impossible.

The function of a government is practically the same as business with the difference being: there is no profit distribution if the entity does a good job. The investors are those who buy the debt (bonds) with an agreed rate of return. The taxes paid by the citizens is the "cash flow" for the country and must cover the expenses of providing security, infrastructure and their management in order to make the first two happen. This is essentially described in the basic functions of The Constitution. This is the foundation of the Social Contract[51] of our government which is "of the people, by the people" for the citizens of a Democratically Represented Republic.

When this social contract is accomplished the citizens can get on with the business of business and make their individual livings. Their profit gives them the economic freedom[40] to spend it in any way they wish. The government was never intended to be a "baby sitter" of the citizens nor should it "throw parties" to attract voters so they can stay in power.

### 5.3 What Freedom and Liberty Means

I attended mass one Sunday where the priest, during his sermon, said something that caused me to ponder the non-spiritual meaning of a biblical saying.

He said the old standard quotation about the evils surrounding the love of money, which I briefly address. He said: "If you love money and ignore your God, you will be a slave to money your entire life. But, if you love your God, you will be free for eternity." This does not need to be explained, but it does make the point regarding faith in a trusting God. God will help you to better survive this life, successfully, through faith in him. But, that is not the point I am making here.

I trust and sincerely believe in God's divine mercy, but the real insight applies directly to our corporal lives in the United States of America. If you extend the logic of this biblical message, this thought evolves:

**If we expect this great country to take care of each us from the cradle to the grave with all the social programs and safety nets that can come from a government, we would be living in the freest country in the world, but we are actually slaves to that government, upon which we depend for everything it gives us.**

This is the epitome of our personal control and self sufficiency that must be exercised by anyone during their life to prevent being enslaved by giving us those things as a means of control.

Freedom can not be possible in a socialist government. Freedom exists only when we learn how to be self reliant and not requiring dependency on a "sugar daddy" government. We can not have freedom without liberty. We are free to do anything we want, but without honesty, fairness and integrity, freedom is not sustainable and we have no chance to appreciate liberty. The difference between freedom and liberty is: liberty has a sense of responsibility attached to it while freedom implies a laissez-faire attitude. Liberty is dangerous without honesty and integrity.

Money does not guarantee freedom, liberty or success. Money is not a blessing. Money is simply a tool used to solve problems. Money only raises the expectations of what is expected and from you individually. The real blessing is in having the talent to know how to use money and other tools we all have to meet those expectations. If one has the talent and does not use it, it is exactly like *not* having the talent in the first place. Any ability, talent, mental or physical skill that is not used is a terrible thing to waste. It is sad if one has any of these skills and has nothing to show for it when they die.

This is a great country. But the business climate, caused by the government in the United State, is among the worst in the world. This is evidenced by the fact businesses are so severely persecuted, yet U.S. businesses often lead the world in almost every thing they do. This is a great testament to U.S. businesses and speaks volumes about capitalism in our system of a Democratic Republic form of government.

This persecution also breeds the temptation by the government "to see how much torture can be inflicted" before these businesses are killed. This is the classic example of: "Killing the goose that laid the golden egg." It is also caused by a lack of integrity, by politicians. It allows unfair practices, described as "Robin Hood" like, to happen. It infects the low information voter (victims) under the disguise of democracy with this approach encouraging the victims to vote in a way that allows these persecutions to continue. Only a lack of integrity in those that vote for or purpose this sort of attitude would cause this to happen.

### 5.4 Balance of International Trade

The connection of integrity to a trade balance is not easily shown as having any relationship. On the surface there is not a relationship. But when it is considered to be a problem, caused by a lack of integrity, the connection is clearer.

To see the connection we must first define the Balance of Trade. The trade balance figure is a bookkeeping entry that shows how much of our manufactured goods and resources were purchased by another country, subtracted from how much we purchased from that same country.

**Balance of Trade  =  Total Imports  -  Total Exports**

We, as citizens, have little interest in this number. It does exposes a symptom that can impact employment, but more importantly it can be influenced by the relative value of each country's currency.

The balance should not be viewed like a box score of a football game.  The difference is: the one with the most points does NOT win.  The best score is a tie.  Whenever it is out of balance there are extenuating circumstances that cause systemic problems.  As in any game, there are rules that must be followed. The reason to keep the score a tie is it influences whether a tariff should be applied and how much of a penalty should be charged to artificially "tie the score" again

There is always a temptation to "put a thumb on the scale" to disguise the imbalance.  This is where integrity comes into play.  Tinkering with currency and product valuations is a hard temptation to resist.  It is easy to do and hard to detect with the risk/reward ratio favorable enough to accept consequences if they are caught.  The lack of integrity is evident by the attempts to cheat with currency manipulations, product dumping or smuggling. After all, what can be done?  Who can blame them for trying? "It is no big deal and everyone is doing it", are just some of the excuses used to cheat.

Like in a football game, the fans can only cheer or boo the players or plays called.  The same is true for the balance of trade.  It is a spectator sport where each player (business in this example) on the field is doing their best to advance the ball up the field with the government the referee

Each company is doing their very best to make things the world wants. These products are for consumers inside the United State and countries outside our borders buy our stuff as well. The companies involve do not really care about who buys their products, they just want them sold.

There is also a side game happening. Like in a football game there are fans who are betting on the outcome. The outcome they desire is to have "their team" score slightly more points than the opponent, of course. There will always be a problem in any betting situation and if there is a way, someone will try to cheat.

In the balance of trade game, there are nationalistic loyalties that causes bettor's to have extreme affinity for their home team. This loyalty causes less than admirable behavior to occur by the country and it is also very difficult to see the cheating when it occurs. The data is on an honor system with the currency exchange rate always fluctuating. This compounds the problem that requires the use of accurate numbers. This can also lead to different interpretations of how to apply them.

The bettor in the trade game is the manager (the president) of that country with the outcome of the game very important in the career advancement of that manager (president or premier). The influence comes in the form of currency manipulation, tariffs imposed, tax law changes and import/export regulations. It is a form of moving the goal post without the other team realizing it until after the game. All these manipulations have disingenuous agenda implications that can artificially influence the outcome. This is the lack of integrity in action. If there was unquestioned trust, the problem would not exist and everybody would gladly do business when the market forces of supply and demand are allowed to work.

But when cheating is involved, market forces are unfairly influenced and will need to be corrected at some point. The consequences may be extreme unemployment, inflation or sanctions that make the original problems worse.

The point is: if the balance of trade is a problem, the problem comes, not from the act of trading, but the deviance of the countries involved to gain an unfair advantage by moving the goal post.

When trade deals are proposed, like NAFTA[80] or TPP[81], the prima facie aspects of these deals always appear to be favorable and profitable for all the parties involved. If integrity were present, what you see is what you would get. But the integrity issue is always the "fly in the ointment", often making matters worse because of the restrictions, limitations, bureaucracies and score reporting to determine its efficacy. The ability to extricate from the agreement if the members are found to lack integrity because they cheated and were caught, is also a problem. There is little incentive not to cheat.

The conclusion is obvious. If integrity is not integral to all aspects of these situations, the result is another problem on the list of the concerns in our world because the agreements only address the symptom......an imbalance in the trade number, in this case.

The situation is further exacerbated by the criticism and condemnation of anyone who would oppose these trade deals. These detractors are classified as heartless, uncaring, against full employment and obstructionist if one is against free trade. All these adjective are usually not constructive, but said to divert away from the subtle influence the bettors (supporters) are hoping will give their home team a slight advantage and win the bet on the game. After all, if they are cheering in the stands and are not involved in the rigging, but knowing the rigging was done, they figure they can't be considered complicit and do not consider it cheating. Again, this is the result of a lack of integrity. They are just as guilty as the manipulator for not stopping the cheating and actually encouraging it by their participation.

## 5.5 Infrastructure

There are only three responsibilities our Federal Government has toward its citizens:

- Creating and managing Infrastructure
- Providing security inside and outside our borders
- Making laws to promote domestic tranquility

These are the fundamental ingredients of the National Social Contract the government has with the citizens of the country. This agreement is an arrangement that is intended to promote sustainability. All laws and regulations are supposed to honest, fair and have no dishonest agenda (Integrity).

This National Social Contract takes affect at the that point where it is beyond the capabilities of our personal contract we have, individually, to society......to make the world a better place by not leaving a mess. We all need to work toward making things run more smoothly. The government's obligation is to do those things that are too difficult, impractical or incapable of being done on an individual or isolated, small scale.

Infrastructure is the description given to all those things used by society to aid in commerce and provide "for the domestic tranquility" as stated in the preamble of our constitution.

The most obvious examples of infrastructure are the roads, bridges, public buildings and the administration of their construction, maintenance and repair. The management of infrastructure requires the investment of tax dollars, not spending them, in a way that will reduce or eliminate future expenses for maintenance and repairs. If they are spent to repay favors or garner votes, this is another classic example of lacking integrity that infects the entire representative government. It has almost becomes a normal expectation of our elective representatives, with that promise the reason they won the election in the first place. They were considered "gifted" at schmoozing and believe they could delivering the goods by bringing home more tax dollars than the constitutes sent in. I once saw a campaign ad in California: "Vote for me so I can bring a larger share of your tax dollars back home."

It becomes a case study of the saying: "The system of democracy will only elected officials who are not much better than the average voter." Jesus Christ would probably have difficulty winning an election without name recognition.

The less obvious infrastructure items are the system of currency, laws and the accounting for these activities. In order to determine a fair way of funding all the infrastructure items there must to a trusted way of keeping score. The fundamental purpose of all these accounting functions is to make the business of government simpler, easier to understand and more efficient as well as providing a system to sustain it for future generations.

> HE IS NOT A LAWYER, NEVER RAN FOR PUBLIC OFFICE BEFORE, NEVER WROTE OR PUBLISHED ANYTHING AND IT IS GOING TO BE REALLY HARD TO BEAT AN INCUMBENT

The function of a business was addressed at length in my first book. By quickly reviewing what a business is, we will make the connection with integrity as explained in the premise.

A business is: that function and/or the activity of making a living. Its fundamental purpose is to solve a problem resulting in a public demand for some sort of goods or services. It is the action of using available resources to provide, directly or indirectly, a source of food, shelter and clothing.

These are the basic items we need to survive. They can be acquired directly, like most people did before the industrial age, by making them. They also acquired other needed items through trading or bartering. The purpose of any business is to make a living (money) with that business existing because it is filling a vacuum or a need in society. If no one wants the item made, there is no demand and there will be no business. No one will give any money for an item they don't want.

The logical extrapolation of this trading system is the introduction of a currency that allowed the "making of a living" function more streamlined, efficient and practical. It also requires an additional layer of trust in the negotiations.

It becomes apparent if integrity did not exist, the basic trust in the value of our currency would not be known. The ability to be compensated the workers making items, without resorting to bartering, would be impossible.

The security part of our infrastructure is not only the military. It is also the law enforcement that reduces the need to spend time fending off simple robbers. This sort protection minimizes interference from intruders by not being constantly distracted fending off threats, trying to stay safe while operating their business. All business would stop if we needed to revert back to addressing the most basic world problems, security. Business and commerce would not be possible if integrity was missing. It would threaten our very livelihood. If no one can be trust because integrity was not there, nothing would be accomplished.

The basis of our tax systems is rooted in integrity. It works only if integrity exists in both the receiver as well as the payer of those taxes.

I have traveled to many countries and saw first hand the customs and traditions of the citizens from these foreign lands. The interesting part is the mindset of those citizens is homogenous in many ways. The reason for seeing these consistencies in personalities and custom is a direct result of their tax laws.

The tax laws in these countries is a game of cat and mouse like a tactical arms race. Practically everything is done with the objective of beating the tax burden imposed upon them. They have various ways of hide their cash and are reluctance to deal in credit or check, even avoiding the use of banks. There is always a suspicion that something bad could happen if they are foolish enough to follow all the tax laws of their country.

They consider their government as untrustworthy and corrupt. They know there is little integrity in their politicians and therefore do not want to be considered a schmuck[82], falling for their tricks of unnecessary disclosure that contribute to the lavish life styles of their politicians or bureaucrats at their expense.

There are numerous examples all over the world where this game of cat and mouse is played. Greece is an example that describes this fundamental symptom of the problem in the European Union. Greece has a great 3000 year tradition of culture which is gradually imploding.

The fall of Greece as a world power started when they tried the experiment of pure democracy. It is conceptually brilliant but fundamentally flawed. The Greeks seemed to forget that a lack of integrity was inherent in everyone. They trusted in the concept that nationalistic pride would cause their citizens to have a near perfect altruism for their country, of which they should be proud.

This democratic experiment worked well for hundreds of years ending with the death of Alexander the Great[94] in June 323 BC. He, almost single handedly, conquered the known world in his short 32 years of life. A simple explanation of what happened: Alexander knew the resources of his country were limited. The only way to grow was to acquire more territory by "taking it fair and square" from the surrounding neighbors.

This approach worked very well as the surrounding areas where less affluent. There was also the charisma of Alexander and the Greek's custom that caused the conquered to be less resistant because of how he treated the conquered. Many surrounding territories wanted to be to a part of a winning team and be considered Greek. The citizens of the surround countryside considered being conquered to be closer to annexation than unwanted aggression. Alexander also showed trust for the conquered. If they showed less resistance, he installed the local officials as the caretakers under the democratic rule of Athens.

The trust he extended to the captured, and the reciprocal benefits, allowing Alexander to remain one of the greatest military leaders in the world. It was said that Julius Caesar, at age 55, had an inferiority complex when he compared his career to that of Alexander the Great.

The concept was brilliant and worked very well for about 400 years starting with the father of Alexander. It was based on integrity. When Alexander died a vacuum, cause by the internal power struggles, evolved into the gradual decline of the empire that gave way to Roman Empire who conquered them. This decline of the Greek and Roman Empires continues through today.

The modern example of Greece is telling. The Greeks have been living on their reputation and tradition with the ingredient of integrity gradually evolving out of their heritage.

Covering the complete history of Greece is found in other books. The point is how today's management of Greece has become the "poster child" for a lack of integrity. The modern Italian Government is suffering a similar fate for the same reasons.

In the mid-twentieth century, the Greek government started trying to "print" themselves into prosperity. They simply put numbers on a piece paper they called money and told their citizens they could spend it. The people of Greece trusted their government when they did this, with the results being inflation that caused the economic disaster the country is now experiencing.

The mismanagement of their currency caused children of the country's farmers to realize life was considerably easier in the city, compared to slaving on the farms. Farm life was hard work and the taxes on the land made it very difficult to survive. The family farm became too expensive to own and not worth inheriting. It became a burden, if they did inherit it, because of the high land taxes. Many abandoned their land as it was nearly worthless because it was impossible to farm it to make any money after taxes. They left the farms and acquired jobs working for the government. These children are now retiring and expecting the pension they were promised, through their service to the government.

The implementation of the European Union caused this unsustainability to come to a head considerably quicker than first anticipated by the government. The concept of a united Europe with a common currency and the synergy of being a part of a larger collective was very seductive. The less affluent countries of Europe, including Greece, wanted to be invited to the party.

Initially this was great, until they realized there were responsibilities that came along with membership. Those responsibilities included stopping the printing of their own money to "pay their bills". They were now required to use real money, the Euro, that had a real established value.

Initially, they did not fully appreciate the consequences of this change. This worked for a while until the pensioners started retiring and demanded their retirement pay. With fewer people working outside the government paying taxes, and the increase in retirement payments approaching the gross national product of the country, it would be impossible for the country to pay its bills. Raising money from some sort of income tax was impossible because everyone was living off of the government who did not have money to pay them. Greece pleaded for leniency, begging to borrow money from the EU to meet their obligations.

This story is replete with examples showing a lack of integrity. The real hypocrisy is now Greece wants out of the EU. The EU wants as many countries in the club as possible. The Greeks are realizing the EU wants them more than Greece wants to be in the EU. This is compounded by "the game" the Greek citizen's play.

The wealthy retiring Greeks are building beautiful home in the countryside and enjoying the pleasures of living in one of the most beautiful countries of the world. But they are not stupid. They also know there is corruption inside their government and they ask: "why pay taxes?" They know the government will take a large percentage to run the bloated bureaucracy, and return only a small percentage to the people. The citizens figure why pay anything as they will only get a small amount back. As a result, no one pays their taxes. The real hypocrisy is the enforcement of tax collection is the responsibility of the wealthy in government who are complicit in not paying their own taxes, so nothing is done with very little money collected.

This is a most blatant example of how a lack of integrity has infected a formally great country with a brilliant legacy. This final implosion occurred over just two generations with the pattern being similar to many countries in the European Union.

There are many similar examples of this unsustainable thinking and is gradually infecting this country as well. The pension problems in California, Illinois and Wisconsin are the poster children of this problem, not to mention the Federal Government acting in a similar fashion.

These examples are intended to demonstrate the similarities that occur when the concept of integrity is missing. This integrity, from having confidence in our currency and having politicians practicing what they preach, is vital. We must all live with true fairness, honesty and the understanding of sustainability. This capability is necessary to have a solvent country for the next generation to inherit.

I continue to find it ironic that all the problems in the world can be summed up in a single word......"Integrity" or the lack of it.

# Chapter 6

## Unemployment and Reason for Jobs

The purpose of any business is, simply, to fill a need. In filling that need it is necessary to coordinate objectives. These objectives will consists of tasks that function under Murphy's Law[12]....anything that can go wrong, will. The things that go wrong are problems that will cost money if not addressed. The true function of a job is not always apparent. The core existence of a job always evolves around problems and that need to have someone solve those problems. Without exception, for a job to exist there must to be a defined problem that is costing money.

If there were no problems inside a business, there would be no jobs. These problems may be as mundane or simple as unlocking the door so everyone can enter or as complicated as determining the minimum sales volume necessary to stay in business. Regardless these issues will cost money to the owner if they are not addressed by someone since these tasks will not happen automatically.

The only real job we have in the world is that of solving problems, and should result in making our immediate surroundings a little better, at least temporarily. There will always be work to do, just like there is gravity that constantly pulls our body to the earth. This force that causes everything to become disorganized, fall, break or wear out must be constantly addressed. It requires energy and effort to do things and someone must always arrange to pay for that energy. People must consume food for that energy and someone must organize the process to have that happen. All this organization does not happen accidentally and problems will arise that must be efficiently addressed.

The only reason anyone is paid for any work is because there is a problem, which is costing money, if not solved. The pay for the worker will always be less than the cost of that problem. If the pay is more than the cost of the problem, the problem will go unsolved or the owner will eventually go out of business. This happens because competition from those who do pay someone less to solve the same problem will make more money if they sell the same item for the same price.

*I ONLY WANT A JOB WHERE THERE ARE NO PROBLEMS*

The jobs that exist inside a business are like cogs in a gear. Those cogs are interacting with other gears. They are addressing segments of the operation that would limit the ability to achieve the basic objectives for the business if neglected. That objective is always to fill a need or meet a demand. For anyone to wish for a job where there are no problems is ridiculous.  The definition of a job is: A task that solves problems.  And the pay for the job is also by definition: it must be less that the expense incurred if the problem was not addressed.  If the pay were more than the cost of the problem, that is not sustainable.  It makes no sense to pay someone more to solve a problem than the cost, if it was not solved.

The real understanding of the definition of a job is missing in most political discourse.  Politicians will often use the populist phrase: "Job Creation" as a way of gathering votes for election.  Saying these words is insulting to our intelligence and exposes the vacuousness of their own intellect.  What they are saying, without realizing it, is they will "create problems" that will require a "make work" job to fix.

It implies that the potential employee is willing to perform a government created tasks to achieve some nebulous objective for a period of time each day, resulting in pay.  There is no definition of what is to be expected.  Just the use of the term "work" to this activity, regardless of anything being done, show a lack of integrity.  The employee is expected to not care what the objective is nor understand what results of those motions are to be.  No one seems to care as long as tax payer money is received at the end of the day, regardless of any noticeable results.  This is actually what is being said when the words "create Jobs" are spoken.

No one seems to realize a job exists only because of problems encountered in the process of making money.  If making money is not the objective, then spending any money that is not tied to a measurable monetary result is wasted effort.  In this case, if money is paid without solving a problem, it must be called what it is: WELFARE.

All money used to provide welfare comes from someone's taxes. The taxes are from income received for solving real problems for an employer who pays them. If money is paid to someone who is not solving a problem, it is making more problems because it is not sustainable and will eventually need to be addressed by someone. Sustainability is a "zero sum" game.

This extrapolation of logic must be understood by anyone listening to a politician who uses these words. The phrase "Creating Jobs" is actually insulting to any business minded voter. It says government must create problems so they can pay someone to fix them. They do not understand the psychology and negative morale of doing some activity for no reason (sometimes called "make work"). This sort of activity is actually harder and unsustainable in the long run.

This sort of activity is a form of the sin of omission and stems from a lack of integrity. Again, it is welfare without calling it welfare. By having someone paid to do nothing is dishonest, it teaches a bad lesson, is unfair and not sustainable. It means one is complicit in the delinquency of that individual. Only a government would act this way because if a business did it, they would go broke. It is not honest or fair and is wasting resources that could be used to solving real problems that make the world better when fixed sustainability.

This explains why government bureaucracies exist. Bureaucracies are not established to address any problem, but address only the symptom of the real problem. By only addressing the symptom, guarantees the problem will never be solved. This gives job security, in perpetuity, to any bureaucrat who manages to acquire one of these positions.

This existence is cause by a lack of integrity, though the entire process, with the end justifying the means. This explains the use of illogical, confusing methods and procedures used in government. It is classic for anyone who has not functioned in the world of "real business", where economic objectives expected and strictly defined.

The mantra of saying we must stop businesses from leaving the country is also classic, vacuous, political remark. Businesses leaving the country is a symptom, not the problem. They leave because of the hostile business environment the government has toward businesses. The government continually tries to raise taxes on business and impugn them for being successful and not paying "their fair share". They continue to impose more restrictions and regulations that incur more expenses and demand the business pay for these items not related to any function in their operation.

They are also subject to "fines and penalties" if the company tires to move off shore. There seem to be a belief that persecution through increasing taxes, imposing more regulations and fines if they leave, will make businesses want to locate in the US. This is the epitome of ignorance and stupidity. The government seems to have a desire to destroy businesses that have real jobs that need workers who want to accomplish something each day by solving problems.

The Government acts as though they have no clue about how businesses run. The fact is the government is doing things that are dishonest, unfair and unsustainable. The politicians only seem to want the short term credit for redistributing tax money. This is the game they play because of a lack of integrity.

All these functions result in exactly the opposite effect, it makes things worse. No business will stay where they are not welcome and deal with persecution at the hands of the government while trying to survive. This is rooted in the lack of integrity by those enabling this sort of activity to continue. It makes no sense and they know it. It is popular to vilify the businesses that are successful. It seem to be a way of seeking revenge on those who are working hard and making money while others, who are made to feel victimized, seem to get permission to stand around, while doing nothing to help themselves.

There are many more votes to be acquired from the low information crowd who are seeking that degree of revenge. This revenge is also seated in a lack of integrity. They know it is not fair, but it is to their advantage to say nothing and take the largesse that inures from the robbery. The more blatant example is riots that stem from civil unrest, with occupy movements and black live matter demonstrations the best examples. They riot because it becomes profitable to the demonstrators in two ways:

1. By the theft of items available in unguarded stores

2. By the pay they will receive in the work to clean up, repair and rebuild the destruction they caused

By not stopping a crime, one is complicit by the sin of omission, which is just a wrong and caused by a lack of integrity. They should be ashamed of their actions and I am certain they would be angry if the stolen items were theirs....again a lack of integrity and hypocrisy. .

# Chapter 7

# Unsustainable Welfare System

The welfare system has its place in society and is an extension of the security system that evolved in the middle ages by kings. It was a way to have safety in numbers, occur naturally, in order to improve the chances of survival.

This started the thought process of social engineering that has always been a temptation of a socialist agenda. They have the conviction that with enough money they could make a utopian world. The part of the analysis that is missing in trying to accomplish their desire: where does our personal contract[52] in society stop and where does the social contract of the government start? Said another way, when is it the responsibility of the country to take care of the less fortunate, how much care is sufficient and who is going to pay for it?

This question becomes blurred because these agencies' have only job: determining an "objective" income level where the government needs to provide welfare assistance. There is considerable incentive for bureaucrats to constantly raise the poverty level. It increases their importance and provides more control over more people who will vote for the party that provides that assistance. This is not honest, fair or sustainable because it lacks integrity.

There are many types of welfare programs being provided: food stamps, rental assistance, energy assistance, cell phones, child care, elderly care, health insurance, crop insurance, and now insurance for pre-existing conditions to name a few. They are all different names for welfare assistance and should be considered only in that way. I have known people who tell their friends they are going run an errand: picking up their "pay check" when they retrieve their welfare payment.

These are all welfare programs that recipients are reluctant to acknowledge as welfare, but there is no other way of describing it. There is nothing in The Constitution saying the government should bankrupt the country by baby sitting its citizens. The phrase "general welfare and domestic tranquility" are being bastardized to imply that it should. We must remember the phrase "We the People". That means all of us are the government and we can not give what we don't have. In the limit, welfare is simply the forced redistribution of wealth. If we each had integrity, the words: "Share and share alike" would be easy to follow. The words: "Rob Peter to pay Paul" is not integrity.

Welfare is the spending of tax dollars to provide a safety blanket for society. The rationalization is these could be called investments and not expenditures because they prevent the larger problem of rioting and looting if the masses rise and demand help because the afflicted perceived unfairness from the more fortunate.

The bottom line is: individual integrity is missing in these programs and their bureaucracies are never ending. They never seem to make the situation better.

As mentioned in Chapter 5.2, the social contract the country's management has with the citizens is to provide the infrastructure, security and laws that are fair, honest and sustainable with integrity. We must also remember the managers of the country are those individuals we hire, through elections, to make sure that happens. This contract goes into affect when "We the People" are not able or capable to do this on a non-collective basis. The result is "We the People" essentially hire a "larger contractor, the government bureaucracy" to do the job. It is impossible for any state or small collection of states to provide an effective, efficient National Defense, for example. Besides, this function must be coordinated on a macro basis for economy of scale to work.

The discussion on the social contract must start where our personal contract stops or becomes impractical. This point involves the function and concept of Federalism[56], determining where the responsibility of individual states stop and where the Federal Government take over. This is also where the difficulty starts.

The natural, apathetic, human condition will try to have the social contract start as soon as possible. This lends itself to a liberal, socialist agenda that favors an early "social contract" involvement while conservative thinking trends toward extending the personal contract for a long as possible with as little as possible government involvement.

The family unit is the fundamental unit where welfare is demonstrated. Young children would not survive without the care and nurturing of their parents. The act of providing food clothing and shelter is a required basic need to have these future adults reach maturity. The responsibility of their parents is to teach them how to fish and not just give them a fish.

The integrity function is to teach these concepts to their children so their existence is eventually sustainable as they become adults. Instead, it seems the children learn how to abuse a system designed to help only those who fall through the cracks. That is what happens when integrity is missing.

Welfare systems have a tendency to evolve into a problem when its administration becomes a mechanism for getting votes. The act of having voters believe they are victims encourages bureaucracies to exacerbate the situation. When they place themselves in the situation that qualifies more people for government assistance, this is laced with a lack of integrity. They are not being honest or fair to the people who must pay for that assistance nor is it sustainable.

The Lord helps those who help themselves is part of this Christian mantra: to be honest and giving to those less fortunate. This is not in the bible but it is true and a good point to remember if we want the world to be a better place. But, if the integrity of the welfare recipient and the bureaucracy providing it is missing and they know it is undeserved, the system breaks down completely and is not sustainable.

The systems become unmanageable and almost antagonistic. The government put bureaucracies together to mandate tax money to support a program that seems to increase the number of poor and needy instead of decreasing the number.

The only explanation for this result is fundamentally a lack of integrity. Their actions are not fixing anything. The only people benefiting are those administrating the program.

The War on Poverty by Lyndon Johnson is the perfect example of a lack of integrity. The naive expectation of eliminating poverty is disingenuous, foolish to suggest and just north of stupid.

Like all contrasts, poverty is on a spectrum. To know what is hot, one must have cold in comparison. To define up we must have down. To understand war we must know what peace is. To eliminate poverty would mean there would be no lower half to the listing showing the net worth for all citizens in the country.

There will always be a lower part. To say we can eliminate poverty means eliminate the bottom half. Let us pretend we can put all those on the lower half on another planet, there would still be a lower half of less fortunate people on Earth. The list on Earth would be shorter but there would still be a lower half of that shorter list. They would probably raise the amount they considered to be "in poverty" so they could keep their job.

The thought that this could be implemented shows a complete lack of integrity and demonstrates why the mere consideration of such an idea is completely vacuous. The fact is the program was not designed to eliminate poverty but spawn generations of "victim voters" who are completely dependent on a government for their existence.

Again, "If you love money and ignore your God, you will always be a slave to money. But, if you love your God you will be free for eternity." This can only be extrapolated to one conclusion: "If you live in a country where one is completely cared for, from cradle to grave, you can be living in the freest country in the world and you will be an absolute slave to the government."

# Chapter 8

## Health Care Costs

### 8.1 Health Insurance and Cost Containment

The reality of life is that everyone must die sometime. The cold hard reality is figuring how many resources should the government allocate to addressing the cost of health care when the results will always be the same.....we will die?

Society is a collection of people trying to make a living to sustain their existence. The need for food, shelter and clothing has been a fundamental requirement for humans over the past 200,000 years of the specie's existence. Over the past 10,000 years we have survived as a species with the security systems of kingdoms, starting in biblical times through the Middle Ages.

The temptation of modern society is to try to include health care as a right. The problem is in defining what "a Right" is. Does it imply that everyone should have as much as they want when they need it for no cost? Is food "a right? Is water "a right"? Is air "a right"? Or does it mean we have "a right" to buy these things when we want them?

If "a right" means society must provide these things for free, who is going to pay for it? The sustainability of this concept seems incomprehensible to those who expect the government to provide it. The compromise of being a society that spends all its money on themselves, while other important projects that would make the world a better place are neglected, is not sustainable. There is a severe lack of integrity being demonstrated if this is an acceptable mindset.

The institution of health care insurance started on the slippery slope of unsustainability in the 1940's. The health care insurance became a pawn in the game with the advent of unions acquiring blanket policies as a part of their labor negotiations. The actuarial analysis of insurance company, providing group policies for businesses, realized it became more efficient and profitable for companies to pay the premiums for their employees instead of giving them more pay.

The normal insurance available individually was considerably more expense than the pro-rata cost pre person in a group policy. The logic was: it was much less expensive to cover the average of everyone in a group policy than for the individual to pay for his own insurance. This difference was a perk that set precedence. It was worth more to the individual than the cost of insurance the company provided. This started the insurance problem that we see today: setting that precedence and having the young healthy people subsidize the older less healthy population.

The unintended consequences of the slippery slope was missed when large Fortune 500 companies were in the throws of union negotiations. This precedence started the thinking that the cost of health care should be included in the social contract of the government to its citizens, as well.

It is important to remember the function of the government, when it becomes involved in the health insurance industry. If they become involved it does nothing in the way of providing better health. It is simply a way of paying for the services provided by doctors and hospitals and becomes a form of welfare. It does not make any one better physically. It simply attempts to eliminate paying for the services of taking care of our own bodies, by having someone else pay for it.

The irony is this does not lower any costs. It only provides more bureaucracy and administration expenses that does exactly the opposite. It raises the cost to unmanageable levels because of the lack of integrity in the process. It violates all the core values of fairness, honesty, sustainability and integrity.

Healthcare lies on the same spectrum as welfare. Both are managing to have these issues considered "a right". The attempt to include "pre-existing conditions" under the business model of health care is not anything like insurance, in spite of what it is called. To cover pre-existing conditions is simply a welfare system called by another name.

When businesses started including pre-existing conditions it started another slippery slope. It set a precedence that was insignificant, originally, and was absorbed into the actuarial analysis of the business. It has now become an expectation that has no place in any health insurance model.

Insurance is designed to spread the cost of a disaster to a large pool that paid for protection from being wiped out if disaster strikes. You can not insure against something that has already happened. You must buy crop insurance before you plant and flood insurance does not go into affect for three months. You can not call the insurance company to insure you home after it burned to the ground. The same thing is true with pre-existing conditions. When pre-existing conditions are addressed, it is a welfare program and any attempt to re-characterize it as insurance is dishonest and lacks integrity.

Insurance has evolved away from a personal contract where everyone does their best to care and provide for themselves, to a form of entitlement under the part of the social contract of this government. This means the personal responsibility of how we pay for our health maintenance is being transferred to "The Government". This is what "single payer"[93] means. The Government pays for everything. The real problem is "where do they get the money?"

The attempt to apply these programs to both the citizenry and to anyone who immigrate into the country is another example of re-characterizing an issue to expand the control of the government.

The liberal thinking is this must be a part of the social contract to ensure domestic tranquility. This is the "Good Samaritan"[61] mindset of the health providers where they will help everyone regardless of their ability to pay. This is "Christ Like" but leads to having the human condition of sharking the system, ripe for exploitation. This would work perfectly if all welfare recipients had integrity. In the end there is a resignation to the fact that: "If they can they will." The liberal thinking is: why not make political hay and use it as a veiled attempt at collecting more victims who will vote for those who advance these unsustainable ideas.

This victimization syndrome is also evident when comparisons are made of how many people will lose their coverage under any proposed alternative. This is also hypocritical. Those that enrolled when the ACA first came out had no option for insurance and/or paid very little for it through subsidies, because of their economic situation. Those who now pay premiums under ACA have huge deductibles making it nearly worthless and almost unusable. The propaganda claiming huge numbers of people will lose their newly acquired coverage, if ACA is changed, is another attempt at creating more victims.

It is similar to comparing how many people can cross a frozen lake without a boat in December, but it is now July. The support of the ice in the winter can not be depended upon year round, so any comparison is meaningless and not relevant.

Nobody had health care that was affordable under ACA, which was not subsidized. The act did not make the situation better. It "addicted" people into thinking they had insurance while not realizing there will be a day where it would no longer be free.

This propaganda were only words used to gain votes from those who can now say they have coverage, where they had no hope of any coverage before. If it is usable and unsustainable, that was never addressed. What will happen when the system completely implodes or how do we cross the lake in the summer without a boat?

The citizens of the United States spends approximately $6 Trillion on insurance and health services annually amounting to about $20,000 per person per year on average. About half of that amount is spent on the infrastructure to provide a place to provide that care. This includes everything from the staffs handling administration, check-ins, record keeping, paperwork, insurance processing, collections and health insurance premiums. How can anyone expect the government, with their additional 10% for their bureaucracy to administer the ACA program, to do it for less? The bottom line is they can't. Government never seems to solve any problem nor did it ever do anything that reduced the cost of something, so it is ridiculous to think they would be able to do it with health care.

It will be only a matter time before the pain of unsustainability will be felt. The lack of integrity by those keeping this fact from being exposed is hypocritical. It is not compassionate, helpful, or constructive nor is it in anyone's best interest to hide these facts from those who now think they have insurance. Sooner or later the "bill will come due". The pain of that bill will be like the pain they will eventually feel when "they fall through the ice" because it could not support those who were on it.

All of these are classic examples of situations with no integrity. If complete honesty were in the hearts of those administrating our health care system, these problems would not exist.

There are needs for assistance in situations that are beyond the ability of individuals to provide for ourselves. It is another welfare system. The argument of whether a government should provide health care brings us to a place where the fairness and sustainability will be in conflict. The motive of those who promote a "welfare type insurance" are becoming suspect as being less than altruistic. These politicians know it causes the voter, who are convinced they are victims, to re-elect them. It does not make anyone more healthy. It only tries to find a way for someone, other than the patient, to pay for it.

The lack of integrity in the administration of health care systems is responsible for these problems. The patient receiving health care is outside the normal business transaction of paying a fee for services and receiving that care. The typical health care transaction today does not follow the normal business transaction model of supply and demand that consists of only two parties. It now involves a contract outside the normal fee for service because there are three or more parties involved in completing any transaction involving health care.

The doctor bill is paid through a contract from a third party, the insurance company. The individual who receives the service is often indifferent to the fee, because he has "no monetary skin in the game". What is charged to the insurance company, who is in a contract with the patient's employer, is the least of the patient's concerns because the patient only wants to feel better, regardless of the cost.

The incentive for the patient to carefully monitor the expenses incurred is non-existent. The hospital and the legal system has every incentive to charge as much as possible without throwing up red flags. The patient's insurance premiums do not go down nor does patient save money by working to reduce the cost of the insurable event. The bottom line is the patient doesn't care about the cost. They just want to be better.

This makes the health care transaction ripe for corruption with anyone involved having their integrity tested. The entire transaction becomes unsustainable with their indifference and carelessness infecting the entire society. It continues to grow further out of control when the government now becomes involved and complicit.

When addressing this from a business perspective, the health care industry will be forced to meet the business expectations of providing health care. The expectation to comply with standard business principles of supply and demand is extremely difficult. There are numerous market forces necessary to insure sustainability. It is impossible to not be considered cold hearted or cruel if the actual human suffering or financial trauma of the situation is ignored.

"There will be dead bodies in the street!" is the cry of the advocates a standard business model health system. They will claim it is impossible to have a business approach be considered because of the impression that business is against any moral standard of compassion and caring. This is not true and spreading this propaganda is another example of lacking integrity.

The government's approach of addressing only the symptom becomes the classic norm of dysfunctional bureaucracies. Any aspect of the patient becoming accountable, or truly interested, is gone. This apathy is human nature which is the result of a lack of integrity. They know it is not the right thing to do, but do little or nothing to stop it. This sin of omission has a dimension where it makes it difficult to sense any guilt, but it is on the spectrum of what is known as a lack of integrity.

Going through the steps that caused this catastrophe is not the purpose of this book. The point is: Integrity is missing. The problem, along with any expectation of finding a solution, is not possible without addressing the lack of integrity. It is more "business as usual" if only the symptom is being addressed. The agenda of creating a bureaucracy trying to fix the symptom is the classic fall back position. The typical approach is to protect the sacred cows with any law designed, not to fix, but to keep the gravy train going. Their attitude toward cost savings or containment is: "don't worry about it as there is a lot more money from where that came". This attitude explains the mantra that the integrity ingredient is missing.

The bottom line of health care is: it is a business and not a right. To expect it to be delivered free of charge or on demand regardless of the cost is not sustainable.

**The problem is determining exactly where the social contract of the government starts and when our personal contract as individual's with responsibilities to society ends.**

Until this is determined there will never be a solution to the health care problem.

A common conclusion is: liberal thinking wants it to begin almost immediately with little personal responsibility while conservative thinking is: the social contract should start only in the extreme, if at all.

Until the point of where the social contract starts, is found and agreed to by a majority of our society, this problem will never be solved. The ability to remove any benefits, that are not sustainable, is nearly impossible with the charge of "lacking compassion", the battle cry. But if this tough love[78] approach is not applies as soon as possible, the entire system will implode and there **will** be "people dying in the street."

This is the same reason the managers of our National Parks post signs that read: "Do not feed the animals." It is cruel to have these animals depend on resources that are not sustainable. It causes extreme suffering and rampant carnage when conditions turn extreme and the unnatural supply of food is gone. This results in the animals having little chance to meet their own needs.

To declare: if integrity were present and everyone in society has health care, the problem would be solved, is not realistic. To find a solution, the definition of what the final result is expected to look like must be clarified. The range of solutions will be somewhere between these two extremes.

1. Have every person in the country paying $20,000 per year to the government so all the people can have free health.

OR

2. Have everyone agree to live by the personal contract and provide their own health care and insurance.

The bottom line is simply how much is each of us willing to pay? Both solutions could work if complete integrity was prevalent in our society. If everyone involved in the process would be fair and honest the costs could be cut in half. This would mean everyone from the patient to the doctor with all the administration who helps provide care, would have to realize their actions must be sustainable and honorable. The real problem is there is little incentive or opportunity, in the current system, to have that happen

If this were to happen, there would still be a need to provide catastrophic coverage if the individual situation exceeded the national average cost (about $20,000 in the ideal case). Again, the cost for providing care in extreme cases must be prudent with a cost sharing mechanism so the patient always has some "skin in the game".

The point that must be realistically faced and the saddest part of the whole health care debate is: The best outcome that can be expected from all this bureaucracy, is we will die healthy with no money to leave for our children's inheritance.

## 8.2 Antibiotics, Organic, PETA[85], GMOs[22]

With the dawn of modern medicine, the technological advancement has given an almost magical world of discoveries and cures that will make the future seem close to nirvana. These treatments and life prolonging procedures make the difference between good outcomes and bad outcomes wider now than in any time in human history. The development of these technologies is a business and must make a profit, eventually, for the development to continue.

The continued development of these technological wonders requires their application be in a business model that has a profit motive. We can not expect the researchers and developers to be perfectly altruistic by devoting their career and/or fortune for little or no profit. It is insulting to one's intelligence to thing this is fair. It is also hypocritical to think the government should force this fate on the health care industry.

There are risks and downsides to anything worth pursuing. The excuses opponents use to impugn business for seeking a profit motive is not constructive and often appears to be a revenge tactic against success.

The difference between good and bad has always existed and on a continuum where it is impossible to not have one without the other. The difference between good and evil in the technology field is very narrow. As stated before in perfecting the problem, we must know hot to understand cold, up to understand down, left to right, war and peace and most of all, we must have life to know death.

It is impossible to eliminate any downside to these comparisons where things are always changing. To eliminate all the problems in the world is impossible. There are always be issues to deal with in life. We must expend energy to overcome the force of gravity to simply exist. As Gilda Radner[11] said in her book, "There is always something".

Thinking all health problems or the possible side affects of technology developments can be eliminated is foolish and naive. The best outcome we can have is to "Die Healthy". The operative word is "DIE" and we need to understand the purpose of life is to deal with this issue. It is on a spectrum which we all must eventually experience. As we discussed, and not necessarily in the order of importance, the purpose of our life is to:

1. Save our own soul

2. Make the world a better place in the process.

Even if one does not believe in the existence of a soul, the second point must apply. Otherwise, your life becomes part of the problem in the world.

When it comes to technology, medicine and the health care industry, we must be brutally honest about what health care is. It is a business that fills a need for something people want. We may think we need it, but in the spirit of being perfectly frank, in the limit the outcome will always be the same. We don't really need health care that is provided by a business, but we all want it and we should be willing to spend our money to get it. The integrity of the situation comes into play when the ones who want it expect someone else in society to pay for it.

The disappointing part about technological advances in science, medicine and health care is: all does is delay the inevitable. The outcome will always be the same, eventually, whether we try to care for our self or we hire it done, we will all die. This is sad but true. There is no free lunch and we must all do what we can to care for our self. The sarcastic conclusion is: we will all die healthy and/or poor, spending our last dollar trying to avoid the inevitable.

Now that we realize the medical industry is business that simply fills a want, we must also realize that it must function in the world as a sustainable enterprise that must make more money than it spends. Any attempt at making the case, there should be "no profit" in health care and must be a right for every citizen, is lacking any sort of real integrity. An individual health care provider can, in the spirit of making the world a better place, set the example of caring for the sick. But it is an insult to anyone's intelligence to think that it must be made available to everyone by a decree of the government for nothing. Regardless of how altruistic one is, there must be some resources spent by someone. The money remaining after health services are provided must be sustainable for future patients after the current patient dies.

Today's technological advances and research must lead to genetic and chemical discoveries that providing better health services. Those findings must be available for all, in an effort to fill a need or solve a problem.

To stop advancements in these fields for genetic research (GMOs) or antibiotics and chemicals, in the spirit of preserving the world, is a form of hypocrisy. All human advancement since the dawn of man has happened because the human intellect insisted it happen. It is part of our own evolution as a species. If we can, we will try to do it. Talent not used is a waste. It is like the man who won the lottery and dies with nothing to show for it. That is a sad summary of that life if that was put on his tomb stone.

To think GMO or technological research must be stopped, is denying the existence of all the advancements that got us to this place in history. To call all the inventions and life simplifying tools we have today as bad, is loaded with hypocrisy. Where is the line that says it has gone too far? When do we stop and put the world in a Mason Jar[23] and seal it, never enjoying the fruits and the marvelous wonders of the world and life? The Biblical story of "The Talents"[24] is only one of several examples where wasting ones abilities and not doing the best we can is wrong and an example of a lack of integrity.

There are generalizations about proponents of technological advancement and scientific study. This does *NOT* mean anyone who supports GMOs, antibiotics or food not considered organic, wants to destroy the planet. A similar generalization is often made about those who believe animals have more rights than an unborn baby, as implied by positions PETA or pro-choice advocates. Both positions can be reconciled if true introspection is made for whether their positions are fair, honest, sustainable and has integrity. When core values are applied, these mischaracterizations will be self correcting when they are applied sincerely.

Those who see the benefits from practical applications from these industries, are not completely heartless and do care a great deal about animals, the environment, and all things in the world. These people are typically the greatest of outdoorsman and environmentalist, working very closely with the land and animals to protect the resources the planet provides. They typically are very conscientious and considerate of those resources, realizing they need to be recycled, protected and not wasted, These resources must be sustainable in the limit for the next generation.

The bottom line is: if unquestioned integrity did exist, conversations regarding sustainability of the environment, industry and health care problems would not happen. There must be a balance between what is fair when determining our obligation to society. The problem that results from the compromising of integrity would not need to be addressed if rules and regulations were actually solving problems. Bureaucratic rules often only address symptoms when cheating occurs and turns into a "shell game" that never addresses the real problem, only what to do if someone is caught. This is because there is a lack of integrity in the system with only the symptoms being addressed.

### 8.3 Disabilities

The disabilities problem is similar to pre-existing conditions problem. Both are unfortunate situations that causes hardship for those with them. These things need to be addressed, including injuries to our men and women in uniform and to our veterans who were injured in their service to our country.

When it comes to soldiers who provide our security for the country, we must put our military in the first place. Their welfare is a big part of the social contract The Government is obligated to provide. We must fulfill our contract to our veterans as it gives us the ability to have this conversation in the first place. If everyone in the country was required to provide a period of service to our Country, the temptation to compromise core values or become apathetic would probably be reduced, if not eliminated.

The same attitude should happen to anyone injured in the process of working and be included in the social contract we spoke of during the health care debate. To provide this social safety blanket would be simple if the system was not compromised by those using it to receive benefits that are not deserved.

The compromising of integrity occurs when there is cheating through claiming faux disabilities that burdens the system with unnecessary expenses. This depletes the resources available for the truly disabled. It is these problems, inside the insurance issue mentioned in Chapter 8.1, which causes the system to breakdown.

The function of any insurance is to distribute the risk over a larger population base. The obvious problem occurs when the takers becomes a large proportion of the group because of cheating. The number of people who are disabled has almost doubled over the past 50 years.[39] This fact alone is a strong indication of how much cheating is happening.

This increase alone is startling. This happened in spite of the influence of OSHA[92] work place rules to enforce safety habits. The expectation should be fewer people becoming injured, requiring fewer disability claim due to greater work place safety. Instead they are going up with more people becoming injured than ever.

When statistic like this are noticed, the cause must be found. The only conclusion is the increased is due to those cheating the system. It has become an expected practice, with one considered a schmuck if one does not take advantage of the "laissez-faire" attitude toward cheaters. There are entire industries[40] built around the exploitation of this segment of health care. The only logical conclusion is the lack of integrity that allows this problem to exist.

### 8.4 Abortion and Euthanasia

The greatest tragedy of our society is the rationalization around the ending a life before it has a chance of starting......abortion by other name. The denial of numerous precedence's from court cases when a pregnant woman is murdered is considered to be double homicide, is an example of hypocrisy. This should be proof of an irreconcilable contradiction in this belief. The denial is a form of hypocrisy that is inconsistent for anyone who has affinity for their own life, much less that of another person, regardless of the age.

The slippery slope of ending a life before it is born, leads to the extrapolation of what is acceptable a few minutes before birth, but becomes a murder a few moments or ten inches later?

If this rationalization is made acceptable, the same logic can be applied to the other end of the life spectrum, euthanasia or assisted suicide. The incredibility of this thinking occurs when there is a complete denial of any scientific or moral conviction, not to mention core values.

It is a direct contradiction to what is honesty, fairness, sustainability and integrity. This vacuous mindset contributes to situational ethics that has gradually infected society over the past few decades. If our purpose in life is to make the world a better place, by leading through example, then the inclusion of abortion, euthanasia or assisted suicide is completely contrary of those core values. The mantra: "we die as we live" are very haunting words when we consider the consequences of these life ending actions.

The position of those who support the allowance of abortion or euthanasia will argue the following:

- It is horrible to have a child delivered into a world where it is not wanted or there aren't enough resources to support another mouth to feed.
- The allowance of abortion has reduced the crime rates in neighborhoods where high population

- densities are causing a complete breakdown of the social structure.
- Euthanasia reduces the medical expenses to the family if death occurred earlier.

All these points have a consistent message that violates the "core values' of any civilized society that truly believes in: Truth, Fairness, Sustainability and Integrity. These excuses for supporting abortion or euthanasia are not examples of great leadership, if one acts on or accepts these reasons for ending any human life.

The inconsistency of classifying these situations as not being a problem is important to note. The actual problem must be determined. Abortion is not the problem, but a symptom that comes from a lack of health care or poor education. Deeper analysis will show the lack of integrity leads to the rationalization that murder of those who can not defend themselves, is acceptable under these circumstances. It contributes to the collection of symptoms like elder and child abuse, pedophilia and various addictions that causes our society to not respect human life or accept the responsibility that come with creating and supporting human life.

This makes it very difficult for a society to stand, survive, thrive or lead if the four core values of honesty, fairness, sustainability and integrity are not followed by our citizens and reflected in the laws they want passed.

### 8.5 Addictions

- **Drugs and Gambling**

When the issue of addiction is brought up, drugs and gambling are the common perception that typically come to mind. The argument that drugs are a physical addiction, while the other addictions are psychological, is a difference without a distinction in this analysis. The actual addiction is the symptom and not the problem.

The definition of an addiction as found in the annals of psychoanalysis is: "An uncontrollable compulsion for behavior caused by deep seated physical or genetic defects that result in emotional, psychological or physical harm to one's self or those close to them."

The consideration of whether it is a societal problem brings us back to the analysis of determining if it is really a problem or a symptom of a problem.

There is little disagreement that addictions occur and the effect on the population is far reaching and harmful. Addressing addiction is an industry onto itself with careers and bureaucracies built trying to alleviate its affect on society.

The standard observation is we all have desires and compulsions. The determining factor, as to whether it is an addiction, is if it interferes or distracts from the performing of expected responsibilities to ourselves, family and/or society. If our obligation in life is to make the world a better place, the self analysis of whether we are living up to our potential will need to be addressed to determine if it really is a problem.

If the brutal conclusion of this self-analysis determines we are underperforming, the question must be asked: What can we do to use more of our God given talents?

The denial in recognizing our potential is the common reaction and a form of procrastination. The world is filled with, so called, underachievers. The under achievement conclusion is most noticeable to everyone, except the individual with the problem.

Again, the premise of this book is to identify the root cause of all the world's problems by perfecting the question, if there is any hope for a lasting solution. When it is defined exactly, the hardest and most important step is achieved when the problem is exactly defined. The answer will simply be turning the question into a statement. When this logical approach is applied, the tendency of addressing the symptom is usually eliminated.

- **Pornography and Sexual Addictions**

To put pornography and sexual dysfunctions into a problem classification under the heading of addictions will cause concern and confusion, not to mention being bias and sexist. This confusion is explained in the premise of this book: "the lack of integrity is the root of all problems".

Sex is a fundamental body function that is primary to our existence as that is the only way to propagate. It can not be controlled or adjusted by laws. It is ridiculous to sanitize it into something that makes it seem "not dirty". The biological function of sex is the reason for everything we do in our lives. We eat, sleep, exercise, work and take care of our bodies for no other reason than to maintain our ability to be attractive to the opposite sex. This is important because it results in children that will need to be raised to do the same thing in order for our species to survive.

If this sexual drive is suppressed, it leads to depression, anxiety, stress and dysfunctional behavior. The degree and extent of these maladies varies for everyone, with different ways of coping with each one. The awareness of when it becomes problematic is a function of upbringing, life style and our value system. This influences how we spend money in an effort to deal with depression, anxiety and stress. The "natural" approach in dealing with these sexual anxieties can be embarrassing or dysfunctional if they are exhibit in public. WHEN this behavior is openly displayed it can ruins careers, reputations, relationships, social dynamics and often friendships. Openly exhibiting these sexual behaviors is not considered normal, with which most people would prefer not to associate.

The act of living, with all our available entertainment options, is seeded in our basic need to function "politely" in society. Everything from the clothes we wear, the car we drive, the movies we watch, the gifts we give, the interaction with our families, the parties we sponsor or attend all have the underlying objective of dealing with our basic and natural function of our lives.....to procreate the species.

Where this natural desire, which is based in our sexuality, becomes dysfunctional is subjective and very individualistic. There is no "one size fits all" remedy to this problem, if it is a problem in the first place. The common ingredient: is the way we individually deal with our desire, the exact way we feel in our heart. If it is, this is a function of our integrity.

How open and accepting would others be of us, if they truly knew exactly how we felt or acted in our most private moments? If these true feelings are different than the perception we would like people to have of us, there is an integrity issue that should be confronted.

Integrity is the virtue of being completely transparent and unafraid of the opinion of others if our true desires are acted out. Any hint of shame is hypocrisy and an indication that we may be contributing to this problem. The act of trying to address this is the beginning of trying to make the world a better place. Like the Chinese proverb "If everyone would keep their own doorstep clean, the whole world will be clean". If each of us teaches our children what true integrity is and live in an exemplary way, the whole world would eventually have the integrity needed to eliminate all the world problems.

Those declaring pornography a problem, did not exercise the problem solving analysis. Porn is not the problem, it is the symptom. The lack of integrity IS the problem. The desire to express ourselves sexually is universal and any attempt at suppression is addressing only that symptom and will make porn more pervasive. "If you want kids to brush their teeth, outlaw tooth paste". This is the classic psychological manipulation used to steer social behavior.

The refusal to accept our sexual existence is a result of the Victorian movement and the hypocrisy of that era.

Once this is refuted, particularly by those who have children, the denying of having sexual desires in their most private moments is hypocritical, if they condemn it as being pornographic.

The act of participating in porn is where the problem becomes infectious. When the participation promotes depravity or the mistreatment of others, is the point is where it becomes a societal problem. The test is simple: "would you be ashamed if anyone found out what you are truly thinking and doing?" If you would be ashamed, there is an integrity problem.

- **GLBTQ**[25]

To classify alternative sexual behaviors as a problem is not the purpose of this discussion. The sexual life style of anyone is their decision as long as their behavior is fair, honest, sustainable and has integrity. The only issue to address regarding GLBTQ is the problem of fairness, if sexual life style is a problem in the first place. Again, the variation in types of sexual desires is not the question. An individual's desire is as varied as personality types. We all have a personality and our integrity will determine how we display our unique personality.

The real problem with alternative sexual preferences is not whether there is a difference from commonly accepted behavior. The problem is forcing us to accept differences in life style compared to traditionally accepted societal norms. If the difference is accepted, it does not stop there because it leads to demands and privileges granted to tradition relationships initially reserved for heterosexual couples raising families.

The problem also discriminates against other single people. The laws and the customs surrounding marriage provides a structure for a society. It served a purpose where there was a need to provide security and structure for the family unit. This is vital for the survival of a functional society.

The family unit is an evolutionary structure based in natural law. It was simply easier and a more efficient way of surviving life to insure the survival of the next generation. The children of any family structure is the most important ingredient in preserving a family unit. Attempts at using existing laws and customs to provide security for relationships that do not produce children is usurping the purpose of the system.

The expectation that any pair of same sex people can seek a legal status that gives the same rights and privileges as that of the opposite sex relationship is not fair. It is not fair to opposite sex marriages or the single people of the world. It leaves room for legal interpretations that could be manipulated into giving advantages found in the tax or inheritance law, previously reserved only for the family unit. In the limit it could allow a father to marry his son for insurance, estate or tax purposes. This exhibits a complete lack of integrity necessary for any law to be considered a "Good Law". The demand that insurance, inheritance and tax treatment be ubiquitous to same sex couples is not sustainable. It is self serving and has no relationship to the promotion of normal family units that has survived and delivered society to this point for the past 10,000 years.

This disingenuousness is rooted in a lack of integrity where the fairness of their demands are ignored. It is discriminatory and actually sexist. The irony is many of the GLBTQ planks, in their platform, are based on inclusion and stopping discrimination of any sort. The very thought of demanding their acceptance is discriminatory and hypocritical. They are single just like any other non-married person. They must live under the same laws as any other single person who subscribe to the belief that a society must preserve the natural family structure to allow families with natural children to survive to the next generation.

This does not imply or in any way suggest, the individuals in non-traditional relationship can be persecuted or treaded differently under that law. This is also not suggesting that acceptance of their non-traditional lifestyle can be forced upon the society as being normal.

This is integrity in action and often the most contentious of the core value examples in play today.

# Chapter 9

# Government Dysfunctionality

The function of government, over the life of this Republic, has evolved away from being a management function for solving problems. It has become a collection of multiple factions, promoting special interests that violate the core values of Truth, Fairness, Integrity and Sustainability.

All laws must contain these four ingredients. Any law that does not have these ingredients is a classic definition of a bad law. The best law is no law with the second best law a law that nobody likes. Laws must address problems and not symptoms. Any law that does not address a defined problem is the principle cause for a bloated bureaucracy with all the "red tape"[15] that results.

The lack of knowing the difference between a symptom and a problem causes this dysfunctionality to occur, hampering efficient problem solving methods.

## 9.1 Problem Solving In a Democracy by Perfecting the Question

For any problem to be solved there is a fundamental principle that must be accepted. This principle is universal in both business and government as well as in life. That principle is:

**There is only one right answer to <u>ANY</u> question!**
(when the question is perfected)

This principle is fundamental to the use of all computers. If there is no agreement on the formulas or parameters programmed into the computer software, the results will not be useful, much less acceptable. It is "garbage in results in garbage out" plus the formulas, values and principles must be in agreement with the participants for the results to be useful. This is done to eliminate any self serving or dishonest agendas from entering into consideration.

The approach to all problem solving requires a full, basic description and understanding of the problem being addressed. Simply:

**If the problem is fully and exactly defined, it is practically solved.**

If these parameters are not defined and agreed upon by all participants, any answer will meet with objections because the solution will probably have unacceptable items in the answer, if not address initially.

Computers originate in a world of absolutes. Everyone agrees on the mathematics and physics laws used and therefore trusts the results. As computers evolved into being used to solve social or diplomatic problems, the parameters gradually became more subjective and less absolute.

For example, "Do you like red or blue?" If the color red was chosen but some of the participants like blue, there will be some resistance. Does the subjectiveness of color become a deal breaker or is a consensus sufficient? The point is: if the color selection needed to be unanimous, that parameter would need to be adjusted for the problem of color preference of the group to have a solution. These preferences could be programmed into a computer with the parameters being a consensus of the majority.

The next step involves a series of subjective preferences. "Do you like big or small?" for example. Is the size more important than the color? These parameters must be ranked in order of importance as well as defining what is big or small, much less what is red or blue. As one can see this "decision tree" analysis can become daunting for humans, but not for a computer.

This approach was the foundation that gave us the true "World Jeopardy Champion". It was not Ken Jennings[29] or Brad Rutter,[30] but the "Watson Computer" built by IBM. This machine beat both, easily. This can arguably be the most important human accomplishment in the history of civilization, even surpassing the feat of landing a man on the moon.

The concept that it could literally replace the function of government and be used to make high level, seemingly subjective decision in business, now seems plausible. Since the beginning of civilization, governments have been trying to do the impossible task of problem-solving "by hand" with solutions that would hopefully be acceptable to a democratic society. Obviously without using the power of computer analysis, it is a nearly impossible task. This explains the slowness of government for getting things done.

The computer was typically used only to acquire or retrieve information for the analysis, but not to give an answer. It was similar to a book with all the information but someone had to apply some logic using that information.

With The Watson Computer, the operation uses ALL the information in the world in attempting to satisfy the words in the question. Watson would rank the most logical answers base on probability. The answer used was the one that best met all the specific parameters in the question. This concept is surprising simple and logical when we envision how we solve problem now, in our head, by hand.

The human limitation of not being able to remember or apply all the known facts and to filter out all emotional bias is very difficult.

This may result in the perception that some preferences, by those interested, were not addressed by that single answer. But if those preferences were ranked and democratically agreed to, the possibility of applying The Watson Computer to address these problems seemed plausible. For example is size more important than color?

The reason monarchs and dictators evolved before democracies is easy to understand. Dictatorships worked wonderfully. The ability to declare an answer to a problem was confined to a handful of advisors with the leader's desires well understood. They got things done by demanding it! But as the concept of democracy evolved, the ability for the king to demand was lost and debate started with everyone one trying to protect their own self interests as well as maintaining a functional society.

The flaw in this concept is the lack of integrity. The voter in a democracy would compromise their own long-term survival in that society for the desire of instant gratification. They sensed the ability to vote themselves "free money" from the treasury. The founders realized this human trait was going to control their actions and they were well aware of the probable outcome. They realized this from past examples of governmental experiments with democracy. The population would vote the country into bankruptcy in two generations, given the opportunity.

The other downside of a democracy is the results of a popular vote insures all the decisions will be, at best, perfectly mediocre. The voting for their politicians and the decisions selected will never be the best or the worst. Their decisions will simply result in the perfectly average outcome being selected. This is because the objective is to satisfy as many people as possible. The further removed from the middle the results are, the more unpopular the decision is with the majority.

The fundamental values listed below are naturally built into our genetics. They appear in every culture in society and are expressed in all religions of the world. They are found in Natural Law [17], the Ten Commandments or teaching in the Bible, Torah[57] or Quran[58] as well as Eastern Religions of Buddhism[59] and Hinduism[60].

### Honesty

Society wishes everyone would be honest. It eliminates suspicion of others and engenders trust and dependability. If this were true we would not lock our doors. All laws contain words that are effective and trusted. If society believes there is a devious alternative or self service agenda involved, it is not honest.

### Fairness

To have harmony in any society, any hardship from a law must not be selective or distributed unequally. If it is perceive to be unfair, it will be ignored or circumvented in some way which breeds anarchy. The best test of fairness is if the parties would still agree if the tables were turned.

### Integrity

Integrity is a concept that causes us to do the right thing when no one is looking or will ever notice. When lacking in society, it causes us to lock our doors and is the reason we have prisons. All prisoners did something which they thought they would not be caught doing. If complete integrity existed our prisons would be empty and locksmiths would be out of business. Integrity also means not pretending to be something you are not. The lack of integrity is the reason dishonest agendas and hypocrisy exists. It means saying and acting the way one truly thinks and feels, and prepared to "stand in front of the firing squad" in defense of that belief if pressed. Politician who make laws that exempt themselves or act in a manner that would be embarrassing, if discovered, are examples of a lack of integrity. Ironically the asperger's syndrome[95] has the identical traits of being completely open and honest about their feeling with no regard for others????

### Sustainability or longevity

Government is a mechanism used to give some assurance that the society will survive and support a standard that is livable for future generations. Any law that does not provide a fair way of funding violates sustainability and is unacceptable, if society wants our future generations to survive. If a law is not sustainable, it is a violation of honesty and integrity and must be stopped.

### 9.2 Principles and Their Compromise

The human element must be considered in this analysis. We all possess traits and feelings that may differ from other members of society. Some are self-serving and others are altruistic. No one with a basic moral compass would disagree with the four fundamental values of fairness, honesty, integrity and longevity. But, we all have preferences that we would like to see in any law. **THE BEST LAW IS NO LAW,** but since we all possess the "human condition" it is necessary to make laws. The next best law is a law no one likes. This is where compromise starts and the part where The Watson Computer comes into play.

Benjamin Franklin said he would never compromise his fundamental core values, but he would compromise on his preferences or, better said, things he would like to see. He realized not everyone can get everything they want and still have a harmonious society.

The implementation of this methodology in a Democratic Republic form of government is the basic reason for the two party system in the United States. The thinking behind our party system is: those with similar preferences will join the group that professes similar principles to their personal choices. We should all have essentially the same core values of honesty, fairness, sustainability and integrity. **In actual fact, the list of differences between liberals or conservatives is actually very small with the only real difference being the ranking of preferences.**

The following is the Logic Tree for Democratic Problem Solving. It makes any law subscribe to this list of **Core Values** that are not subject to Compromise.

## Decision Tree Analysis Problem Solving in a Democracy

**Premise:** Define the objective any law is trying to accomplish in the form of a question.

Any problem has only **ONE** answer if the problem or question is stated exactly or perfected.

Any law must pass through THE 4 TRUTHS or filters and not be subject to compromise.

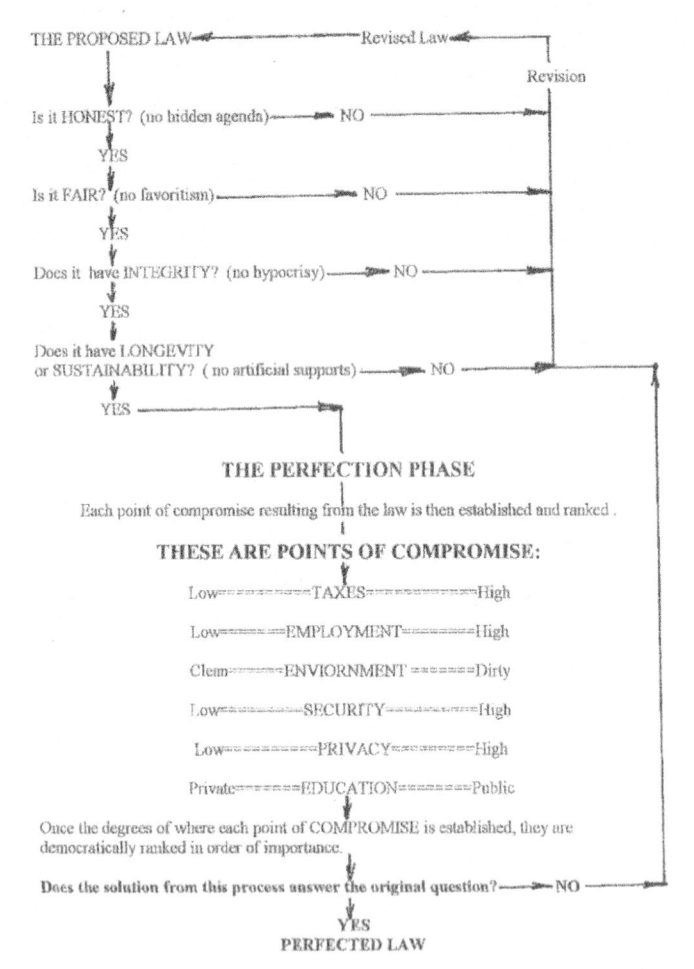

```
THE PROPOSED LAW ─────────── Revised Law ──────────┐
            │                                        │
            ▼                                     Revision
Is it HONEST? (no hidden agenda) ──► NO ───────────►│
            │                                        │
           YES                                       │
            ▼                                        │
Is it FAIR? (no favoritism) ──► NO ────────────────►│
            │                                        │
           YES                                       │
            ▼                                        │
Does it have INTEGRITY? (no hypocrisy) ──► NO ─────►│
            │                                        │
           YES                                       │
            ▼                                        │
Does it have LONGEVITY                               │
or SUSTAINABILITY? (no artificial supports) ──► NO ►│
            │                                        │
           YES ──────────────────────────┐           │
                                         │           │
```

### THE PERFECTION PHASE

Each point of compromise resulting from the law is then established and ranked.

### THESE ARE POINTS OF COMPROMISE:

   Low========TAXES==========High

   Low========EMPLOYMENT=====High

   Clean======ENVIORNMENT====Dirty

   Low========SECURITY=======High

   Low========PRIVACY========High

   Private====EDUCATION======Public

Once the degrees of where each point of COMPROMISE is established, they are democratically ranked in order of importance.

Does the solution from this process answer the original question? ──► NO ──►

YES
**PERFECTED LAW**

# FLOW CHART OF WATSON LOGIC

In the logic tree of any computer program, if a law or position violates a core value, the analysis stops.

Additional data, in each area of compromise, is needed for a computer program to give an acceptable solution. The parameters for each issue must be defined, measurable and agreed to for the analysis to continue. Once the values for each issue are established, the list must also be prioritized, in order of importance, for the analysis to proceed. The approach is not getting everything we want, but what is the least we would accept in each area to reach an acceptable solution.

As difficult as this seems, it is considerably easier than working on an answer, floating a solution for review and criticism, only to have it rejected if a part of the solution is not acceptable to some smaller segment of the participants. Every solution will have its critics, but if acceptable limits or standards are established, the solution will more likely be acceptable.

In actual fact all problem-solving and debate regarding business, social, domestic or international issues uses this approach with the solution, a result of attrition and/or fatigue, not logic. The need to experience this "birthing" procedure is inescapable with the only limitation of a computer analysis being the answer will come too quickly and easily. Without the pain and suffering of analysis and debate the results will be difficult to believe and/or trust.

I have a friend who helped his father run a local grocery store in the 1960's. The Christmas season required the obligatory display of trees placed outside, out of the sun, on the coldest side of the building. He was always the designated "tree service representative" to help the local housewives select the perfect tree. The patron would invariably quickly select one tree and set it aside and then continue to want his help surveying the entire lot for another potential "more perfect" tree. After 45 minutes of standing in the cold, moving trees around with other work waiting inside, the customer would almost always pick the very first tree she spotted and set aside. It seems to be human nature and will never change unless the pain of the decision making process is experienced.

The objective problem solving model, using the capabilities of a Watson Computer[41], eliminates the problem of the human condition that rejects simple answers when they come too easily. Having a Watson Computer available would be very helpful, saving considerable time, money and eliminating the mistakes of unintended consequences. But unless all the agendas programmed in the computer are honest and have integrity, the best of all the resulting answers will not be accepted. Without the computer, the best answer is often rejected because someone did not get something for their disingenuous agenda. This is due to their lack of integrity by not wanting their true motives exposed in the initial input, which they were ashamed or reluctant to express.

The conclusion from this analysis when dealing with any societal issues, it will simply take longer without a computer. The birthing process seems to be required. Once the initial step of agreeing on all the core value issues is completed, the second step, the settling of the preference items, may be contentious but at least it should be peaceful.

**The only reason to ever go to war is when the above approach stalls in the core value phase. If there is no agreement on what is Fair, Honest, Sustainable or what Integrity is, the only alternative is forcing the loser to comply.**

After the winning a war, the process will continue to the "preference phase". Hopefully the result is harmonious for the society that won as well as the society that lost.

The idea of a cold war is a result of not coming to terms after the hot war. It is usually an "attrition" strategy where the losing side feels it is more advantageous to not settle the question and sneak around the issue, rather than addressing it once and for all. This is another classic example of a lack of integrity and only delays the inevitable.

All the cease fires, truces of cold war actions are the lingering results of unresolved issues with the strategy of buying time to mount a stronger offensive. The lack of integrity in these issues in rampant with the objective to keep "the embers of anger" glowing for future generations, so they can continue the cause some other day when the opportunity presents itself again. The situation in the Middle East along with the civil rights movement and border wars in Europe are all examples of this.

There is a need to keep the anger over the perception of being victimized by past generations. This is primary in these cold wars. It is often the only way the older generation can inflict their desire for revenge. The aspect of "settling" where no one admits guilt, but agrees to pay something, is usually the best they can expect. It is often used like blackmail, where the problem doesn't go away, but temporarily postponed. The most troubling part of this process is the afflicted, often, does not want the issue resolved. The issue is their identity and without it they do not have a cause, no matter how unjustified it is.

### 9.3 Political Agendas

The reason political parties exist is the same reasons we need to have words to describe contrasts for everything in our lives. Like we pointed out, there are degrees to every condition. We must agree on the extremes of all these conditions, to know what position is acceptable. We must describe, in relative terms, what is: cold to understand hot, up for know down, peace to understand war. The contrast between political parties is used to describe the difference between a liberal[27] and a conservative[26].

A conservative is typically known to have affinity for the status quo or "business as usual". Their reasoning is the current methods of government operations exist because they gradually evolved into being and work reasonably well. It seemed to be the best so far, with any changes made a result of a desire to gradually perfect these methods.

A liberal is known to favor quick changes that border on experimentation. Their thinking is: the process is too slow and the need to modernize is necessary. Conventional ways of doing things are all questioned with the thought of unintended consequences ignored. The Revolution in American and France in the 18th century experienced this with liberals calling it the Age of Enlightenment[43] resulting in their respective revolutions.

There is a paradigm shift occurring when differences describing liberals and conservatives. In Revolutionary Times[28] those that supported The Crown[31] were considered conservatives, with the word "conservative" not yet coined. Those supporting the overthrow of the British Rule in the new country were considered liberal and radical with their followers called "Revolutionist". The irony is the Founding Fathers of this country were very liberal with very radical views that were not seen as workable much less possible.

I am certain most liberals feel exactly the same way today, with their convictions strongly rooted in unfairness and discrimination. These feelings are not unlike our forefather's feelings toward The Crown with their desire to have a "Democratic Process" for managing the country.

The hypocrisy, or lack of integrity, starts with the liberal agenda thriving in the idea this country is a pure democracy. As described before, a pure democracy has never existed in the United States. The concept of majority rule is seductive as they see it as a way of social revenge where those that "have" can be robbed, if enough "have nots" vote to steal it. The integrity requirements of honesty and sustainably are missing because they soon run out of rich people from whom to steal. The fairness issue is further perverted as they attempt to place the responsibility for all of the past atrocities against the Native Americans and/or Blacks on the current generation of those who committed the atrocities. This is a classic example of unfair reasoning: punishing the son for the sins of the father.

The fact you can not justly condemn the son for the sins of the father, applies in the abortion issue as well. Imparting punishment on the current generations for past indiscretions is wholly illogical. Integrity and fairness would dictate that responsibility must lie only with those who perpetrated these terrible acts and not to their off spring.

As shown in the "Watson" solution of solving problems, the integrity ingredient is factored into the programming where the bias from a compromised integrity is filter out. This gives a nearly ideal solution with the possibility of unfairness, dishonesty or unsustainability filtered out in the process of being objective.

Obviously there was no "Watson" computer around at the time of The Country's Founding. The founders also realize the inherent danger of a pure democracy and the democratic process, so the Electoral College[89] was invented. The objective behind the invention is pure genius. It defaulted to positions that are more honest, fair, sustainable and have integrity. But the real genius of the Electoral College is: it is almost self correcting. It limits the possibility of human nature tendencies that stop our core values from happening. It makes it more difficult for dishonesty and unfairness to corrupt our system with a "mob rule" sort of government that occurs, in the limit, as the result of a pure democracy. It is a check against those who do not have a fair, honest or sustainable expectation from their government.

The aspect of "Term Limits"[90] has a less obvious connection regarding a lack of integrity. A typical liberal agenda prefers change with "term limits" extrapolating into being an obvious change agent. The thinking and logic surrounding the movement originated in the observation that politicians were becoming "fixtures" in legislative branches of government. The result of these so called "fixtures" was a government that was resistant to change, lacking new ideas. The propaganda constructed around this was: a lack of change was not good. Therefore to improve the situation regarding the making of laws, limit the amount of time anyone could serve in that legislative body.

This movement is ripe for corruption and the introduction of disingenuous agendas. The machinery of government is complicated, requiring some "practice" to be effective at it. In the early part of any politician's service in office, they depend heavily upon career administrators that serve at the pleasure of that office holder. The newly elected official is reluctant to fire anyone when they arrive, because they need help finding "the restroom".

These administrators along with career lobbyist find it considerably easier to influence a new office holder than a seasoned politician with years of experience. This results in more liberal laws being introduced and passed with the "naive" support of the new politician who is on a very steep learning curve. This often has unintended consequences that a more experience politician would notice and stop before it reached the point of no return.

The bottom line is term limits become a "Trojan Horses" that quietly allows laws to pass that do not have the ingredients of fairness, honesty, sustainability and Integrity. The only way to get these sorts of laws passed requires a "change agent" in the legislative branch. This is considerably easier and faster than the next change agent called judicial activism.

### 9.4 Supreme Court and Judicial Activism

The fact that judicial activism exists in the United States is a prime example of a lack of integrity. It is hypocritical if the concept of "blind justice" exists in our legal system. The thought that laws can be crafted with consideration for political correctness or situational ethic is abhorrent to our system of justice.

The concept that: "The end justifies the means" is the slippery slope that has infected practically every generation in recorded history. It is rooted in political correctness that evolved into situational ethics which is subliminally finding its way into our legal system. This entire infection can only be blamed on a lack of true integrity. This is not hidden from the people who manage to survive the political gauntlet of election. They must survive this hazing to be in position for appointments to powerful committees in our Federal legal system. Judicial activism is the symptom resulting from liberal activist gaining positions on these committees who filter the acceptability of nominees.

The thought that liberal or conservative influences can affect the outcome of issues that come before the courts is frightening. It leads to future laws being influenced by bad precedence from past rulings. These decisions morph into rulings that undermine the spirit of the law by parsing the letter of the law.

The far reaching conclusion: there is an undermining of the trust in the idea that "right will prevail". This has destabilizing affects upon the laws on which we expect to have the four core values. The idea these decisions could reverse principles rooted in the Ten Commandments or even natural law is very unsettling and not sustainable in a society where there is an expectation of a secure future based on precedence.

The temptation of using the court system to implement policy is a symptom of political correctness and another example of a lack of integrity (hypocrisy). This is outlined in Alinsky's[54] book the "Rules for Radicals"[55]. The problem is not the judges, they are simply tools used by the activists to circumvent the establishment and implementation of laws. The irony is they "bask in the glory" of democracy but are implementing their ideas in ways that are anything but democratic. Another violation of what is expected from those having integrity.

For activism to have any possibility of working, requires a very long time line and the patience to be persistent. The biggest problem that activism has: it needs victims who are indoctrinated into thinking they are being abused and neglected. The need to have a villain that is defined and obvious is very important for the propaganda to "have legs". Propaganda is formulated from factual statement but re-characterized by the insertion or deletions of a few words. These tactics are necessary for the above ingredients to be consumed by the low information voter so they will be susceptible to this bad method of law making.

It is an example of mob rule where their understanding of democracy is: those who scream and yell the loudest, while intimidating any dissenters, to get their way. The activist also has no concept of the hypocrisy they display and no regard for fairness. Would they accept the same thing if the tables were turned? It is another example of the dishonest mantra, "the end justifies the means".

Activists are convinced there needs to be restitution for the behavior of past generations against the ancestors of present day victims. This victimization is necessary for the elevated emotions of perceived unfairness to continue. They must keep the unrest simmering to achieve their objective. This entire conversation would be moot if the core value of integrity were truly present in today's activist, because they would know it violates all the core values. The people who gain positions, that are supposed to have the public's trust, should never violate the core values inherent in good laws.

### 9.5 Tort Reform

The function of the legal system, with integrity, is to have the spirit of the law prevail in all disagreements. The objective of "your day in court" is to make sure the less articulate and experienced individuals in our society have an honest and fair chance of receiving justice with "all men equal under the law" the guiding principle.

The system has evolved into an arms race where the simple process of litigation is made to be considerably more uncomfortable and expensive. The concept that an alternative remedy, outside court, could be sought is practically non-existent. When fairness is upset by money or connections, the possibility of receiving a fair decision is nearly impossible. The defendant will "do the math" and realizing it is cheaper to pay some amount that is considerably less than the possible penalty, if the legal system ran its course.

This is wholly unfair with no integrity found in the entire process. The process of reforming the legal process is equally fraught with pitfalls and hazards. This reformation becomes a legislative issue with a large number of representatives, who are lawyers involved in the legislative process, allowing it to be what it has become. Their careers, and that of their colleagues, would be adversely impacted if the system were fixed. The solution should have the prosecutor that losers in nuisance lawsuits pay all the expenses of the hapless defendant.

This all comes to the same point we have been finding through this entire narrative. The lack of integrity is causing violations in fairness, honesty and sustainability that seem to matter little in the litigation process. The tort reform example again demonstrates where the symptom responsible for all this expense and injustice, is caused by a lack of good integrity.

# Chapter 10

## Bureaucracies: They Never Solve any Problems

The word "bureaucracy" is an outgrowth of the formation of committees to address issues inside a bigger entity. It can be likened to a cog in a wheel where each cog is necessary for the wheel to rotate and deliver power. These government department (bureaucracies) should be able to problem solve the issue for which that department was named. The reason they never solve the problem is they have not perfected the question about their problem and have no concept of what the final solution would look like in the greater scheme of things.

The function of committees are familiar to anyone who has worked in a non-profit or social structures designed to accomplish the production of an event or gathering. They are subsets of civic groups or churches to raise money or celebrate an event. Committees are usually temporary and dissolving out of existence at the conclusion of that event or project.

In the evolution of government these committees spawn into entities known as bureaucracies. They tend to become the "perpetual" as they maintain the symptoms of any problem they address, compared to an event that occurs and ends when the objective is met after the social function concludes.

Bureaucracies have a trait unique to any animate object. It is the only living object in the world that never seems to die. They are perpetual and self sustaining with their only purpose seeming to be: "never solve any problems" but just keep the infrastructure going.

There was a situation where government technicians were found to be still working on the Y2K issue, 17 years after the fact. Since bureaucracies normally exist to provide a service to the public, their motive was to show effort was being made on solving the potential problem. This is another example where integrity from those involved should not have allowed this to happen.

Integrity and defining the objective is much more important than the accomplishment of keeping a "do nothing job". The natural tendency to resort to a model where only symptoms are addressed, while important and pressing social issue are only studied, becomes the standard procedure of these bureaucracies. But, once these bureaucracies are formed addressing the symptom, they can never solve any problems as that would compromise their "eternal life". They would be eliminated if the problem they were assigned to solve, disappeared.

Bureaucracies are fertilized and born through a lobbying process designed to address only symptoms. If the problem is ever identified, it is immediately smothered. That revelation would be a death knell to their existence. The common missing trait through this entire process is the ingredient of integrity.

If that element was added to the process, the problem solving process would identify the real cause of that problem, as demonstrated by the "Watson Computer" problem solving procedure. The symptoms would be identified as noise and the root cause of any problem would quickly surface.

When the actual problem is identified the resources needed to address the issues are usually finite. The need to address recurring funding is often overlooked in the problem solving process as they are not necessary.

This concept seems mystical and unrealistic, because it is. It is unrealistic because the concept of unwavering integrity never occurs, especially if there is a group assigned to address the problem and does not address sustainability.

There are usually one or two individuals with integrity in these groups, but they will be shunned or marginalized and eventually eliminated from the team, if integrity is missing. This, again, demonstrates a bureaucracy will eliminate and destroy any hint of integrity if it jeopardizes the bureaucracy. This same situation occurs in countries ruled by dictators.

The objective of this dialogue is to explain this observation so the trap, that is always lurking, is quickly identified and eliminated. The longer a bureaucracy remains in existence the more difficult it is to eliminate it self.

### 10.1 Global Warming

There is not a person on this entire earth, with at least some integrity, that has any desire to harm this planet or the environment in any way. I will concede there are those, with less than sincere motives, who will stretch those boundaries and be less than honest in taking care of the limited resource we have on this planet. But there is also a tendency, inside these bureaucracies, to condemn anyone who does not believe that the climate is changing because of human influences. This is closed minded and they are guilty of the very sin they condemn, lack of tolerance and a science denier.

The selfish activity of wasting and abusing natural resources, not the affect of greenhouse gases[32], is the most harmful activity to the planet. It is an order of magnitude more serious than the production of $CO_2$ and the concern about global warming.

For activists, blaming global warming primarily on human activity is a crucial to have any hope of their environmental cause to "have legs". This strategy is caused by a lack of integrity and fraught with hypocrisy......again with "the end justifying the means".

There is no question the planet is going through climate phases with the "news cycle" for these changes lasting about 20 years from my personal observations and studies as an engineer. I have seen the beginning in the late 1960's where there was alarm the world was cooling and a new ice age was dawning. I was involved in the acid rain controversy until it was shown to be a hoax because all rain is naturally acidic. (It is necessary for rain to be slightly acidic to breakdown and dissolve rocky material for new soil.)

The proof that man made greenhouse gases are causing the destruction of the planet will not be discussed here. The perception this is true, with no real data, makes the anthropogenic connection the greatest hoax in the history of the planet.

If anyone has a position on the issue, the conviction of which side one is on, is solely a function of integrity by all parties. If one believes that man made global warming is true, does not automatically give the right to trample any other law that is fair, honest and sustainable. Using global warming as a valid reason or excuse to enforce wealth redistribution is simply another way of stealing.

## 10.2 EPA[33]

The atmosphere surrounding our planet is the shield that protects each of us from the fatal results, if we were exposed, to the environment of deep space. The air surrounding our planet consists of a cocktail of gases that has evolved over the past 3.5 billion years. The mixture of those gases have resulted in a layer of insulation as well as a "food" source for our bodies and plants, to symbiotically survive and have sustainability. The air we exhale is the air plants need to survive and visa-versa. This balance is beautiful with life not possible without our fifty mile thick layer of air.

The need to protect our environment goes without saying. But putting a governmental bureaucracy, the Environmental Protection Agency (EPA), who has little incentive to solve the symptom, is a problem. The problem is caused by a lack of integrity which may not be obvious.

The EPA, inside the Department of Interior, is one of 15 executive departments: Agriculture, Commerce, Defense, Education, Energy, Health and Human Services, Security, Housing (HUD), Justice, Labor, State, Interior, Transportation, Treasury and Veterans Affairs. The reason for any of these departments to exist is to administer oversight. This is to determine what rules to make, we call laws. All this in an effort to stop what they consider to be causing problems that department is supposed to stop.

In looking at the above description, while considering the premise of this book, it should be obvious the existence of these departments never solved any problems. The problems seem to be getting worse and costing more money to operate while accomplishing little.

The bureaucrats are only trying to manage by addressing the symptoms that are causing these issues. If integrity and trust existed universally, both individually and/or collectively, these problems would not exist.

The reason I am picking on the EPA, is that agency is the easiest example to show how a lack of integrity is making the concerns about the environment a tool to advance a dishonest agenda. That agenda is based on wealth distribution and population control which seems consistent with most liberal positions when taken to its logical limit.

This is not an attempt to expose a conspiracy or to accuse anyone of aggressive attempts at dishonest behavior. The reason I am making these observations is these dysfunctionalities are deeply buried in our society, because of political correctness. The result is most people do not realize the consequences of these attitudes or that their actions are caused by a lack of integrity.

To demonstrate the hypocrisy of the global warming movement, it is necessary to go under the umbrella of the EPA and their though process. Some simple calculations, that are easy to understand and extrapolate logically, will show the vacuousness of their thinking. This is the inverse of the false mantra used to by alarmists to justify the existence of a man made problem: "Coincidence does not prove causation." The inverse would be: "a lack of incidences should prove no causation."

The validity of the numbers comes from the same 97% of scientist who claim global warming is man made. Whoever these scientist are, will agree with these numbers because they are measurable with the predicted outcomes being: no increase in the number of major storms, no substantial sea level rise, no melting of the ice caps, no decrease in the number of polar bears or proof temperatures are any higher than the were 20 or 50 years ago.

None of the predictions of climate alarmist have come to past. That should give some indicate of who's data is superior. The following number are validated because they indicated none of the above mentioned "disaster" have happened.

The greenhouse gases (GHG)[34] in our atmosphere consists of five components [33] at sea level:

- 70% Water Vapor and dust
- 15% Carbon Dioxide $CO_2$
- 10% Methane $CH_4$
- 10% Ozone $O_3$

Carbon dioxide ($CO_2$) is the only substantial man made component that results from the burning of fossil based fuels. Water vapor and ozone do occur but are more or less innocuous. Almost all the other components occur in our atmosphere naturally, with negligible amounts from human activity.

$CO_2$ has been selected by the environmentalist as the cause of atmospheric temperature increases causing the gradual warming of the planet, in spite of it being less than a 15% component. But $CO_2$ is also the only controllable component attributable to man so it becomes the designated scapegoat. $CO_2$ is a very necessary component for life as it is used by plants in the photosynthesis process. $CO_2$ is also exhaled in all breathing processes.

The fact that is conveniently overlooked: only about 10% of the 15% that is $CO_2$ in all GHG (1.5% of the total) is due to anthropogenic (man made) causes. $CO_2$ is slightly heavier than air and becomes a smaller component at higher altitudes and therefore contributes less to the greenhouse affect in the stratosphere. That is where the GHG shields the planet from dangerous solar radiation of outer space along with the earth's magnetic field. Water vapor and dust seem to be the greatest contributor to the GHG affect with the ability for man affecting magnetic field of the planet being impossible. It is probably the same probability as man being able to affect the GHG component of our planet.

To conclude that $CO_2$ is the "smoking gun" simply lacks any logic or credibility when these facts are considered. All the propaganda on Global Warming is usually anecdotal focusing on the results *if* the planet did continue to warm. Since Al Gore[35] produced his movie in 2005, none of the predictions in his movie have come to pass..????

An interesting observation is: unless we were told that the climate is warming by "climate scientist", few of us would notice or have any first hand observations the climate is changing because of man. All this public support is based on hearsay.

The inability to substantiate environmentalist claims fundamentally shows a lack of integrity. All the accounts of warming evidence are from written reports that told us the climate is changing. The most interesting observation is none of the predictions that should have resulted from these changes have come to pass. There is no sea level rise, no shrinking ice caps, no diminishing polar bear population, no increases in tropical storms, none of the concerns that would provide any credibility to their claims have occurred.

Even the claims of average temperature is suspect, due to inconsistencies in how past data was collected and how the current readings are made in comparison. If the high tech, "extremely accurate" thermometers of the past were mishandled touched or breathed upon before the reading or if it was place in a general proximity of any heat source (a chimney for example) would influence the readings, both in the past and currently. The extreme care needed in collecting data for historic purposes is also suspect. The importance of accuracy is at least an order of magnitude greater today, for the data to be useful for a valid comparison. The entire process is fraught with errors that were not considered as important at the time.

Another fact, conveniently overlooked, is **IF** all the ice on the North Pole melted, it would have NO affect on the sea level. Just like when ice melts in your drink, it does not raise the liquid level in your glass. Ice floats and reduces in volume when it melts with no change in the volume of the water it displaces when it was floating.

If all the ice over the south pole melted, volume over that land and not floating, is about 3% of all the ice in the world. If that ice, only over land, melted that would raise the level of the oceans by less than 6 inches. If all the ice on the North Pole melted, it would contribute nothing to raising the sea level because the North Pole ice is floating. This is not meant to discourage anyone from doing everything possible to conserve and recycle all our resources, both natural and man made, but be aware of the lack of simple scientific reasoning behind these statements predicting doom.

We must all do our part to make this world as clean as possible, because it is a greater crime to not conserve or recycle. We must all do this in spite of the fact it will not affect the rate at which warming occurs naturally. We must all conserve and recycle because it is the right thing to do and not be blackmailed into doing these things.

The oceans are warming as a result of the earth's atmosphere gradually warming, naturally. These cycles have always occurred. The abilities to quickly and more accurately study these phenomenons is now available and the temptation to extrapolate conclusions is irresistible. Validating this data is a great source of funding for continued research and study, if believed. The lack of integrity is at the heart of this entire issue.

The coral reefs around the world are showing signs associated with the rise in ocean water temperatures. This is concerning to all of us and will need to be studied. They should be studied, as that is part of our process in making the world a better place. If all the answers to the secret of the universe were known, it would be a very boring world with no natural puzzles left to be studied or figured out. This is the brilliance of creation and will always leave questions and mysteries to investigate.

The ultimate objective of this research should be to understand the "why" of all these phenomena. The temptation for researchers is steer the findings, not for scientific advancement but for exploiting situations, is dishonest. To raise societal concerns, is hypocritical if used only to gather more funding to do more studies. This integrity issue explains much of the alarmist concerns we see with the attitude infectious, creating even more alarmist concerns, keeping the industry going.

There is a man made island the size of Texas in the middle of the Pacific Ocean made entirely of floating plastic. It congregates there because of the natural eddy of the ocean currents. The hypocrisy is this is a huge environmental disaster in the making and impacts everything from food packaging to the petroleum industry. About 5% of all the petroleum produced is used to make plastics, but that 5% never goes away and continues to accumulate. The fossil fuels, on the other hand, are eventually burned and go into the environment which is where nature intended it to go as part of its natural cycle. As explain before, that amount of plastic is significant and is continually accumulating. We all need to do our part to minimize putting this plastic byproduct into our atmosphere. Global warming is actually a minor nuisance compared to the environmental impact of plastics.

Plastics are the real environmental disaster of the world today. It is one of the by-products of fossil fuels. This is, by far the greatest threat to our environment and animal life on the planet. These petroleum based, non-natural products produce a material that is practically indestructible without burning. This is not the case for the Green House Gases. Nature tries to break down plastics into smaller and smaller partials. This does not destroy the molecule, but makes is more likely to be consumed by birds and fish that will eventually kill them. It clogs their system or disrupts the body chemistry as the body tried to assimilate this man made compound. Plastic requires the high temperature of combustion to destroy and return it into a biodegradable product in order to make safe, again, for the environment.

Plastic should be treated like a hazardous waste and either not produced or made so expensive that no one will throw it away. It must be recycled or handled by a "refund of the deposit" paid when purchased. The integrity needed to implement this process is critical as it will require effort and a lot of inconvenience to be successful. There are entire industries that exist around the use of plastic, either in manufacturing or packaging. These would be disrupted if the requirement of eliminating plastics were enforced. The integrity involved in having this occur would be monumental. It can be accomplished only by having the comparison of not dealing with it being more painful than the loss of profits in changing how we use and handle plastics.

This modus operandi, ironically, is the same for "plastics" as that of the global warming movement. The difference is the group size of perpetrators for the "plastics" movement.

The perpetrators in global warming movement are the deep pockets of industry. In the plastics movement the perpetrators are everyone who uses plastic. The victims of "plastics" movement are the same group. Are we, as a society, willing to inflict the pain of dealing with the plastics problems on ourselves? It is unlikely but hypocritical if they won't. The ability to inflict pain on a smaller group of global warming villains is considerably easier, forcing them to submit and change. The global warming movement uses a form of "Black Mail" to advance their agenda. In the plastics movement, the victim and the perpetrator are the same entities and it would be our own selfishness, as a society, if not addressed more aggressively.

The hypocrisy (lack of integrity) in the Global Warming movement comes in the form of spreading the propaganda of fear. They base their conclusions on the extrapolation of temperature trends. Everything goes in cycles, but by instilling fear that climate change is causing "the sky to fall" is a form of lying. This causes the argument that we "can not take a chance by doing nothing" to justify the liberal agenda that is anti-business and pro-population control.

Saying "we must do something" is in an effort to instill a greater sense of urgency. Using our children as victims if nothing is done increases the sense of urgency. It is a complete lack of integrity, particularly if the result causes personal enrichment to the messenger. The money gathered with this message only goes to additional research, not to addressing the cause. There is no correlation between the research and actions that result in changing the climate. Anthropogenic warming is highly improbable with a greater likelihood it is probably impossible for man to impact the temperature of the planet in any way.

As mentioned previously, if they solved the "faux" problem of Global Warming, there would be a lot of "crow to eat" and a lot of so called "scientist" would need to get a real job. The bottom line is there is considerably more money in the perpetration of the hoax than having it solved. The other hypocrisy is the world is told the United States is the main perpetrator since the US economic production shows we produce about half of the GHG ever produced. Therefore the international community feels the U.S. we should pay considerably more money to clean it up. That is in spite if it even a problem in the first place.

The United States is currently considered to be the second largest contributor (25%) of GHG, producing about 7 billion tons per year in 1995. China is the largest at 28% but about half the amount per capita amount of the United States because of China's large population. In 2015 the US produced about 6 billion tons. It has been estimated the

United States spent about $20T since 1995 in efforts to reduce $CO_2$ by about 15%, yet the amount of carbon dioxide in the atmosphere has continued to rise from about 280 ppm to over 350ppm.[36] Where does all the $CO_2$ come from if U.S. industries are producing almost 1 billion fewer tons per year? It does not seem to be possible that it is coming from the industries in the United States, but the United States is expected to shoulder a disproportionate amount of the cost to curb $CO_2$ production from industries.

By further analysis, showing how many BTUs[62] from the burning of fossil fuels that are added to the atmosphere shows the improbability of human activity being a contributing factor:

The solar flux on the planet is estimated at $1 \times 10^{24}$ BTU/yr. The Energy from all fossil fuel burned each year is $1.3 \times 10^{17}$ BTU/yr. This ratio (1 to 8,000,000) is equivalent to a can of beer in a 10 lane Olympic swimming pool/yr. This ratio is about the same as the amount of man made $CO_2$ produced by fossil fuel per year compared to the entire biosphere.

If the natural temperature variations, from winter to summer as well as the difference in temperature variation from the northern and southern hemisphere are considered, the anthropologic influence becomes more incredible because the man made fluctuation is so small in comparison to nature.

The difference in solar flux varies about 7% from winter to summer everywhere on the planet. This is because of the change in distance between the earth and the sun as well as the slight wobble of the planet as the earth experiences seasonal changes. These natural changes are nearly an order of magnitude more in the amount of energy the earth receives from the sun compared to any human influence. It is approximately the difference between the heat from a single paper match, to the heat from a 10 watt light bulb at the distance of 12 inches. If the matches was lit and held by the 10 watt bulb, the addition heat felt at 12 inches, from the match, would be nearly impossible to measure. The same affect is occurring in the global warming model with man made warming equal to single match held 12 inches away......almost negligible, if any amount.

The bottom line is man made $CO_2$ is not the "smoking gun" and in turn neither is the United States. There is no doubt that the world's climate is changing and these changes have been occurring for millions of years. This issue would not be on the "radar screen" if there was integrity found anywhere in the process. It is a self-servicing scheme of wealth distribution in an effort to slow the American economy so other counties can extract money from the United States. It is used as an attempt have other countries better compete against the United States and gives the U.S. a handicap, allowing other countries to catch up after being disadvantaged for generations. This disadvantage was because of their energy limitations that hindered their ability to compete on the world stage, not to mention the effectiveness of capitalism.

Again, this is not encouraging the wasteful burning of fossil fuel or waste of any of our natural resources. We all must conserve and do our part because it is a sin to be wasteful. We must all set a good example for the next generation because it is the only right thing to do.

If there is any good resulting from the man made global warming hoax, it has caused society to become more aware of the "sin" of being wasteful of any of the "gifts" this planet gives. If the "scare" of global warming caused us all to be more careful, that is good. But, I have difficulty justifying the movement because: "the means should never justify the end" and if it does, it is a fundamental lack of integrity in action.

### 10.3 Fossil Energy

The aspect of energy in our society ranks fourth on the list of necessities to maintain life in our civilization, behind, air, water and food, all of which allows the species to procreate. The sources of that energy varies from our own muscle strength for finding water and growing food, to the burning of carbon based materials releasing the energy stored in those hydrocarbons formed by the sun. Even the oxygen in our atmosphere has the sun involved in its formation.

Practically all energy sources have their origin from the sun. The production of wind, hydro, wave action and of course solar energy requires the energy from the light and warming affects the sun gives. This fact gives energy the perfect focus giving a single a single point where nearly everything could be controlled. The only other major control point existing today is the internet.

Without the energy from hydrocarbons, society would be reduced to the Stone Age existence of our distant ancestors, although, they did depend on the burning of hydrocarbons, both fossil and non-fossil, to survive.

The need for energy puts society in a precarious position if anyone has the desire to control any other faction of society. It can be a weapon of war.

This control stems from the manipulation of our core values: fairness, honesty, sustainability and of course, the most important one is integrity. With the energy issue a point of vulnerably, it is nearly impossible to prevent mass destruction if malicious intent existed from a foreign power.

No one can control the sun, but the agenda of global warming is the perfect tool to do the next best thing. To propagandize the agenda of anthropogenic global warming (man made) through energy, it becomes the best way to control society. To instill the idea that man's very existence is in the balance, is a powerful tool. This lie causes society, though political correctness, to fear our fate if something is not done to stop the world from warming.

Since we can't control the sun's ability to burn its fuel, to imply the blanket affect of our atmosphere is being compromised is the only remaining option to exercise that control.

The real agenda is to perpetrate the belief that society is too big and the ability to co-exist is not sustainable if we continue to propagate at the same exponential rate. This population control concept is laced through all liberal agendas. Abortion, birth control, GMOs, organic food, chemical uses, energy control and industrial growth concerns are all used as tool to advance their cause. They all directly impact population growth and are inter-related.

The desired outcome of this agenda is a socialistic system where everything is equally distributed and consumed accordingly. When this happens, the expectation is nirvana with an equilibrium that would be perpetual. All the world's problems would be neutralized if harmoniousness would exist. This is not realistic to expect and nothing close has ever happened when attempted, always ending in failure.

The concept of this expectation having any chance of working directly violates the fundamental core values of fairness and integrity. This is not be the internal desire, in our heart of hearts, when there is cheating and rules that are not applied equally. We would need to compromise fairness, truth and sustainability to achieve an outcome of socialism in a society. We all have a free will and have a desire for our families to survive. The family will always take precedence over the survival of a stranger.

The real irony is: socialism would work if integrity existed inside everyone. The reason socialism fails is the tendency of "free loading" becomes unsustainable. The reason capitalism has worked better than socialism is: capitalistic systems are built around the human desire to achieve and logic which is the basis on the principle of "supply and demand" and "survival of the fittest". Socialism, on the other hand, is manipulated by taking away incentives to achieve and violates all the core values.

### 10.4 Nuclear Energy

The irony of the nuclear energy dialogue, this is the only source of energy that does not come from our sun, but from the radioactive elements created long after the "Big Bang"[37] and technically referred to as star dust.

Nuclear energy alleviates all the environmental concerns resulting from the use of hydrocarbons. Because of this fact, the ability to control society by the methods outlined, is not possible if nuclear is used to provide all our energy needs. The result is the solution that addresses all the environmental demands of society, but almost universally rejected as dangerous.

The same agenda is used to limit the attractiveness of nuclear energy. The exploitation of the fear, through safety concerns along with the permanentness of its residual by-products is the classic ploy. It plays on fears of the unknown, just like the global warming agenda.

The liberal agenda to control society is the driving force of their agenda. All energy options needed for our existence have consequences that are not necessarily problems but issues that need to address and controlled. There is always something undesirable or objectionable in selecting any of the various options for energy generation. Eliminating all risk from various approaches, developed from our very existence as a species, is difficult. But it is the responsibly of all of us to be practical by realizing there is risk in everything we do. The expectation that all these different energy generating activities must be completely free of risk and eliminated, if a very slight risk exists, is simple minded, short sighted, naive and impractical.

The core value of sustainability, with nuclear energy, is its greatest advantage. Sustainability, with the other three core values, will bring us back to the premise of this book.

When true integrity exists in the analysis of environmental concerns and when the continual examination of our own heart is practiced through our example in how these decisions are made, the concerns of the world would be eliminated......sounds like something Jesus would say.

### 10.5 Immigration

The issue of immigration along with all the other associated terms of racism, acceptance, diversity and family values are also being hijacked and perverted. This is done to advance an agenda of power and control.

We are all individuals with an individual identity and a free will. The immigration problem, when it "lumps" individuals into groups, is racism. The individuality is eliminated and a victim class is created. The need for these groupings is vital to advance these agendas, as the pro-immigration agenda needs a common cause that can be used to disseminate mantras and talking points for the victim class to believe and spread. This in turn gives greater power to deliver votes in the election of these politicians. This result is the advancement of an agenda that lacks integrity and difficult to maintain or sustain.

Most members of a group realizes the lack of integrity in their message. Addressing these inconsistencies, as in a group cause, are overlooked, individually, because they are too busy making a living and taking care of their family to lobby aggressively against these inconsistencies. It is especially easy to be apathetic if they sense a monetary gain is a result, in spite of it not conforming to core values.

The ability to carry this message without exposing the inconsistency is very difficult. If that message results in some advantage, the advantaged will gladly go along regardless of any unsustainability or hypocrisy. They will appreciate the short term benefits and rationalize their allegiances by associating with "the crowd". They escape individual criticism of a less than honest agenda by their association as a group. This mindset is contagious with generations assuming a belief that 2+2=5 with no reason to question it as long as the entire group feels the same way and the benefits continue to inure.

This group psychology in the immigration issue gives permission for any member to compromise their individual integrity with the short term reward of doing so. This far outweighs the long term benefits that would result from learning self sufficiency and individual dignity.

### 10.6 Education

For education to be on the list of societal problems, the definition of what exactly is the problem must be determined. Typically the problem is defined as "not enough education" is being provided for the next generation. This is not the problem. There is more education available today than ever before, so providing more education would probably not solve the problem. The real problem with education is the product produced (the student) is not able to function as a contributing member of society. There is a disconnect between the acquiring of knowledge and trying to use that education. Today, it is difficult to justify the cost, with the false belief they will earn more money because they attended school.

The bureaucracy involved in providing this education, is lacking integrity. The education process is being used to advance an agenda. The institutions receive more funding to provide it but the schools are not able to increase any retention or improve the application of the education being provided.

The analysis of the education system can be further simplified by perfecting the definition of what education actually is. It is not the acquisition of information by an individual. This makes about as much sense as picking apples but leaving them in the basket to rot. Students are not paid for what they know, but for what they can do to solve problems in the world. I believe a student must be able to explain what problems they are going to solve in the world before they deserve a diploma in high school. If they can't, they missed the reason they were in school in the first place. College would be a complete waste of time and money if they can't answer that question in high school. I always had a difficult time knowing what problem an "art history major" was going to solve in the world.

This is the definition of education. IF it does not solve a problem, that would mean the act of only gathering knowledge, with no expectation of sharing it, is education. That would be wasteful, selfish, foolish and counter productive.

For education to be worth something to society, it must be shared, taught and lived. If this does not happen, it is useless. It is part of the definition of leadership where an individual's actions become those that set an example for others to follow by making the world a better place.

In the case regarding education, the integrity question that causes education to be on the list of problems is a result of the dishonest agenda. Education is being used to advance that agenda of spreading liberal propaganda and has little to do with education. Education is only being use a tool to provide a forum. The Trojan Horse here is: it is politically incorrect to object to anything relating to education. When this happens the sin of omission is in play. It is considerably easier to go along, rather than explain the paradigm shift necessary to see the error of this thinking.

Education is not the problem, the lack of any concept of how to apply it to make the world a better place by solving problems is the problem. Not agreeing with this is another classic example showing a lack of integrity, not to mention fairness or sustainability.

# Chapter 11

# Dysfunctional Social Intercourse

### 11.1 Fake News Phenomena

The evolution of how the compromising of integrity has infected society is evident by the way the name of this phenomenon has changed over history. In Biblical times it was simply called "a lie": The expression of something as fact to gain an advantage or deceive someone in an effort to protect or avoid an undesirable outcome of a situation. Today the "political correcting" process of a lie is now more politely called a "non-truth". This softens the accusation, making the charge less painful for the accused.

As we evolved into the age of the printing press, information was able to be printed en masse rather than slowly written individually by hand. The ability to have information more widely distributed for public consumption allows information to empower the individual. The word "non-truth" also evolved to be a more politically incorrect word, so the word "propaganda" was coined during the revolutionary periods of the 17th and 18th century.

In 1928 the ultra liberal agenda of U.S. Socialist Party's also used this political correcting process. They realized their party would never gain popular support with the word "Socialist" in their name. This was due to the horrible economic track record countries with socialistic governments had, so they changed by associating with the current Democrat party.

Their logic was: The U.S. has a two party system and to have any hope of advancing their socialist agenda, associating with Democrats made good sense as their position were very similar, just not as extreme. This is a perfect example of the saying: "Would a rose by any other name smell as sweet?"

> THIS IS WHAT
> SOCIALISM SMELLS
> LIKE, TRUST ME!

This change in name was simply an attempt to justify the means to a desired outcome for the revolutions they were advancing. It was considered acceptable to "spin" the situations in society. To advance their agenda has a sort of "arms race" mentality. Injustices from the ruling class, where they considered themselves to be wrongly oppressed, were exposed and exaggerated. This was done to gain traction for their position

This thought process has evolved, more pervasively, in the age of TV and radio. The wealthy private interests and corporations, with the help of Madison Avenue advertising and the media, guided opinions. This propagandized their agendas, with the help of the major three networks. The products they advertised made people want things they didn't know you needed. They also realize that people only listened to news with which they agree. So it was important to "prepare the ground" by controlling the agenda they wanted advance so the public would hear only that news and information that supported their liberal positions.

With the age of the computer and the internet the ability to spread this information, right or wrong, has further empowered smaller groups of special interest. They use the same modus operandi to advance beliefs and positions that have less altruistic agendas in the form of what is now called "fake news". The construction pattern of fake news is: to ask questions or take a poll where the wording forces a "false choice" to be made. If the interviewee acknowledges either false choice, it is a sound bite.

A subset of this fake news phenomenon is the term "astroturfing"[66] or the claim a movement has large popular support while being fabricated by a small, smart, sophisticated groups that operate behind the scene to advance a fringe special interest.

Sharyl Attkisson[63] gave a TED[64] talk at the University of Nevada, found on YouTube, outlining the problem this is causing. It is causing our society to evolve from one that knew little about everything at the middle of the 20th century, to a society that knows a lot about nothing with much of that information completely wrong. The ability to filter this information has become a challenge greater than the old challenge of getting any information about a topic in the first place....during the age of The Encyclopedia.

Attkisson advocated that we watch for four signs or indicators about any information. This occurs in advertising, mainly from the internet, indicating one should be suspect of the validity of their claims.

1. The use of inflammatory terms like pseudo, prank, nutty, lie, paranoid, quack or conspiracy. This is a typical indicator that their claims are to be highly suspected as unreliable.

2. The claim to debunk a commonly held fact as myths about studies that were actually well founded on scientific research. Then propagating a myth of their own, with their research from surveys and not actual studies done by reputable researchers.

3. Attacking and challenging the groups who formulated the initial scientific findings as self serving and bias, not the issue these findings showed.

4. Expose skepticism of those who show skepticism. Said another way, they do not question authority, instead they question those who do not question authority of the establish standard.

There is some good that comes from the exposure of the "fake news" phenomena. It is now much harder for major media outlet to shape the liberal agenda. Fake news has always existed, but now it has evolved, making it more difficult to monopolize the agenda. In the recent past, the masses followed the major media outlets which coordinated their message with the governing body they wanted in charge. Now that social media has gained some influence, it requires each of us to make a greater effort to think and logically conclude concepts, independently.

Today's society seems to know more about nothing than anytime in the history of the world. This lack of knowledge and the major media's ability to control the message, makes it ripe for radical movements to gain traction. This is a classic ploy used in WW II Germany and describe in Alinsky's "Rules for Radicals".

The irony and hypocrisy of the "fake news" phenomena, it is not new nor a phenomena. It is the rebranding of the word propaganda by another name. The anger and fear of losing control after elections that rejected failed policies is the driving force that causes and orchestrates this newest craze. This is how a lack of integrity is responsible for the situation to be so out of control.

They insult the low information crowd by using different, non-threatening words to describe ideas through which the propaganda of socialism, like a Trojan Horse, attempts to advance their cause in a subversive way.

In these times of fake news, there are tendencies to extrapolate observations by making conclusions that are the least favorable to their opposition. This is done to impugn the integrity of those individuals. When the extrapolation of any activity leads to a conclusion that has never happened before, in spite of the very low probability of having that conclusion happen, is how this propaganda "grow legs". When the propaganda mill continues to report a nearly impossible conclusion, the only perception the public can make is to consider it as fact, in spite of having no basic in fact.

Which is more likely to occur for any individual: doing something with no record of ever committing that act in the past, or an individual **not** doing something for which there is an extensive history and reputation for committing? The latter is considerably more likely. It has always amazed me when a high profile individual is caught in a compromising situation, the first remark that is made: "I have never done that before." The truth is: This is the first time he was caught doing that it.

Paul Shanklin[69] made the observation: "The easiest question to answer for a politician is the question that can not be asked." The question that can't be asked is the one where there is no inconsistency found in their actions or behavior. Integrity is acting exactly as our internal emotions dictate, always, and with no one having any grounds to ask the question to suggest something different. This speaks to the integrity of the media as well the way the media plays their "interview game". This game is played constantly with questions where there is no desire for an answer, but for a sound bite that can be used, out of context, to embarrass or impugn the interviewee.

The advent of modern political correctness in the United States appeared sometime after WW II with the civil rights movement. It did exist before but in a form of radicalism. The things considered politically correct today, were taboo in the past and too outlandish to be considered credible.

The segregation of the races and the discrimination against fellow citizens is a horrible practice. They may have a different appearance, customs and ancestry but that difference is not grounds for exploitation. This stems from a mindset of condescension and/or superiority.

This attitude became irreconcilable when there is no concept of fairness or honesty. The human inability to forgive and forget becomes a difficult pill to swallow. The internalization of this attitude causes a latent hypocrisy to infect society which is another way of saying a lack of integrity....the state of ones heart where one refrains from acting out or expressing their true feelings.

Segregation is not unique to this country or to these times. Racist attitudes are laced throughout history with some evidence found in prehistoric studies in the evolution of the species, Cro-Magnon and Homo sapiens. It is thought the latter possibly caused the former to become extinct or interbred making it difficult to distinguish any differences. There is also evidence in the animal world of species, very closely related genetically, but not able to integrate with each other. There is a species of black ants that appear to be very closely related to red ants. In spite of having the same mannerism, they are not able to cohabitate in close proximity with red ant colonies in the same small area.

These facts are not intended to express any concept of justifying segregation, but there seems to be latent tendencies found naturally in our society where sometimes "we just don't like someone". But to have these baseless feelings about someone, through no one individual's actions is simply wrong and ties back to a lack of integrity. Not liking someone is a form of segregation, appearing on the same spectrum. The point is affinities are subjective and difficult to explain. To deny this is an example of a lack of integrity.

As the segregation movement gathered momentum, the understanding of how unfair it was, is becoming readily apparent. To advance their cause, the need to educate the children and inform others of the evils of segregation has become more acceptable and expected. Whether this was constructive is questionable because it seems most racist people are those who constantly look for example to exploit to impugn and condemn as being racist.

Making stereotypical conclusions of personal behaviors of various groups, is racist. The anti-racist movement seems to be a hypocritical and blind giving total acceptance of everyone's behavior, regardless of how deviant or dysfunctional that behavior. This gives roots to the concept of political correctness. The favorite tool is to associate this politically correct attitude as "Christ Like" and a sin if one does not accept everyone else. This acceptance is expected, in spite of their poor social behavior and their actions to do things that are dishonest, unsustainable or unfair to others. This is a result of political correctness where it is not acceptable to criticize. The hypocrisy of their agenda is: accept everyone who looks and acts differently as long as they all believe the same thing.

The exact definition of "political correctness" is nebulous with Google defining it as: "The avoidance, often considered as taken to extremes, of forms of expressions or actions that are perceived to exclude, marginalize or insult groups of people who are socially disadvantaged or discriminated against". The point with PC: it is now acceptable to tell other people it is "not nice" to criticize someone for their actions regardless of how dishonest, dysfunctional or unsustainable. The irony of the "PC" attitude is if one disagrees with their position, there is no limit to what is acceptable in confronting those who disagree.

We would think this was a good thing and society would benefit from this blind, unquestioning acceptance. But, of course, when taken to extreme it grew to the point where nothing is unacceptable. It has come to the point of being admirable for anyone "to have the courage" to act in an unacceptable fashion.

With nothing unacceptable, it gave subliminal permission to do or act in anyway they pleased without being judged or reprimanded. This can be liberating, but without accepting the responsibility for our individual actions, it becomes unsustainable, hypocritical and dishonest. The problems it inflicts on other parts of society leaves people, who are trying to make the world a better place, with the job of cleaning up the mess. This is the very essence of a lack of integrity where the self-centered, careless activities are inflicting systemic problems that any individual with integrity would realize was harmful in so many ways.

Another consequence of the political correctness, that infects us, is the failure to recognize there is the "sin of omission": The tendency to leave a key word or fact out of a statement, completely re-characterizing the conclusion or impression of the statement.

The political correct influence occurs when there is the desire to not offend or become involved. The PC excuse is they are reluctant to elaborate on a situation or discus things because it will require additional explanation or proof of their words that may be uncomfortable. Also, not wanting to involve others, who know the same information, is also committing the sin of omission. By not saying something is being complicit and accepting of the wrong doing.....and almost as serious as committing the wrong act.

The extreme example is not stopping someone from being assaulted. This inaction is practically the same as if they are participating in the assault. A more common example is when someone votes for a candidate who is less qualified and possibly corrupt because they would be enriched if they win, instead of the more qualified, honest candidate.

A more subtle example would come in the form of "Gossip". Gossip by definition: casual or unconstrained conversation or report about others involving unsubstantiated details not confirmed to be true. There is some confusion in society, with the impression that just talking about someone else is gossip. This is the wrong impression, that comes from the "political correctness" movement.

Talking about someone, if it is true, is a social convention that puts a check on bad behavior and is actually constructive. If bad behavior is not impugned, it is a sin of omission. By not pointing it out as wrong, one is actually supporting the wrongful act. Someone with integrity will point it out and that is not gossip of one does so.

These acts of omission are the most prevalent ways of compromising ones integrity. By not saying the truth, allowing dishonesty to continue, when the opportunity to stop it is not used, is a lack of integrity.

To preserve ones integrity is not a simple task and requires courage and determination. No one said it is easy and nothing worth doing ever is. This is the main reason they crucified Christ. He was the epitome and the best example in the history of the world of someone with ultimate integrity. Some people in power do not like that thought and we all know how that turns out.

**11.2 Poverty**

The aspect and realization of the condition called poverty is subjective and usually defined by bureaucrats who are charged with trying to solve a perceived problem by only addressing the symptom.

The issue of poverty has been around since the existence of humans. The gathering together of several families was the most practical way of surviving, realizing communal living was more reliable and efficient than the individual trying to survive independently. Whenever there is more than one of anything the immediate tendency, by human nature, is to compare. It is the foundation of the theory: "The survival of the fittest"[44] and no matter how hard one tries, the tendency to *NOT* compare is practically impossible to eliminate.

Poverty is actually a state of mind. The definition comes from sociologists who must classify and group things for comparison and study. If someone is in the middle of a large, sparsely populated region, completely self sufficient, and not making much money, they are not in poverty. They have the ability and means to find adequate amounts of food and water to provide a comfortable, sustainable existence. They are self reliant and not dependent on anyone else for their survival.

In spite of the fact they have no currency income, that is not poverty. They are living in an area where wealth is not measured by money. It may be as simple as having one less arrow used to hunt compared to his neighbor that could determine relative wealth. They live where self sufficiency makes them richer than someone with a lot of money who can't do anything for themselves.

Poverty is that designation given by a bureaucracy designed to try to eliminate the condition. This is impossible. Fifty percent of all doctors graduate in the bottom half of their class and there is no way to eliminate half of anything, unless everyone is perfectly equal. This is impossible to accomplish except when everyone is tied for first place.

The statement in the US Constitution that all men are created equal means we are all equal under the law. "WE THE PEOPLE" determine what is Fair, Honest, Sustainable with Integrity (no false agenda). It does not mean we should all have a nice car, the same amount of money or able to buy the same goods. It means we have free will to do what we want, independently. No one can be limited by any law that precludes certain people from certain things, because of who they are, individually, under the law.

As soon as poverty is used as an identification tag, the compromising of our individual integrity is being threatened. It means there is a perceived unfairness that is to be exploited or addressed, by a bureaucracy, to make inequality disappear. It never solves the problem. IT only addresses the symptom of unequal wealth. The prescription to solve this symptom is to eliminate the inequality by redistributing their money to those in poverty making them feel a little wealthier.

There are no adjustments made for ability or effort. It is an objective reallocation that is supposed to never change. It is not possible to make it static, any more than we can stop the day from turning into night. These bureaucracies can not, nor do they want to solve the condition of poverty. That would put them out of business and out of a job. There is more incentive to redefine the condition to find more victims in the poverty than to solve it. The incentive is to classify and entice more "victims".

The bureaucracy needs to keep them voting for those politicians that support these programs of continuing their efforts at the redistribution of wealth.

### 11.3 Crime

The aspect of crime being a problem in our society usually goes without questioning. Obviously people do things that are "against the law" with the adjective, criminal, assigned to them. We hearken back to those days in Catholic school with the Baltimore Catechism and the section on the definition of a mortal sin. It accurately defines crime: It must be grave or serious and committed with full knowledge that it is wrong and with the full understanding of the gravity of the offense.

With the premise of this book being: all the problems in our society are symptoms caused by a lack of integrity and not actually the problem, it follows that crime is also a symptom that is caused by a lack of integrity.

As with sin, there are degrees of everything. Theoretically, a lack of integrity is not a crime. A crime is committing any action or activity that is unfair, dishonest or unsustainable. Integrity does not have a universally acceptable definition but, like pornography, I can't define it exactly, but I know it when I see it.

In the definition where unfairness, dishonesty and unsustainability are mentioned, these are the effects that result from a lack of "good" integrity. The concept that we must force ourselves to do something different than what our heart desires, is a lack of integrity but it does demonstrate self control if one does not always act on one's feelings. If we do what we should do and not what we want to do, this is the opposite side of the same coin. The spirit willing but the flesh refrains.

As with a sin, we must know the difference between good and evil with the social norm being that of the natural law. We, theoretically, have been programmed to do fundamentally good things by these natural laws. These "good" things evolved through natural selection as good traits. This caused this natural law to be a survivor and a good example of how survival of the fittest delivered our civilization to this point in time. It was a desirable trait that caused good to prevail.

Our prisons are filled with people who committed crimes they did not think they would be caught doing. Almost without exception, the act they were caught committing was not the first time they committed that act. It always amazes me when some high profile individual is caught doing something less than honorable. The first thing they claim is: that was the first time they ever engaged in that action. But, again, in the deep recesses of their heart, they would admit it was not the first time, but they first time they were caught.

There is another self correcting aspect that causes one to be aware of exactly what is integrity. The Catholic Church has a sacrament called "Confession"[38]. The institution is brilliant in its concept and based in the roots of The Bible.

The wisdom of the scholars who wrote The Bible realized the concepts I am trying to express here. It is the fundamental message Christ was trying to deliver while he lived. Integrity is the foundation of a sustainable society when all the individuals in that society have a "free will". It is a daunting responsibility for each of us individually. The fact is a lack of integrity is the basis of all evil and is the fundamental reason for all the problems in the world. That it *can* be put into a simple message is surprising and needs to be constantly repeated. There are, obviously, numerous problems still existing in the world because so many people are still not getting the message.

The rationalization that "ignorance is bliss" is one explanation for apathy. There is a continual effort to seek forms of entertainment to distract us from being aware that problems even exist. It explains addictions and dependencies along with all the recreational options constantly being presented on all the media outlets. Movies, Sports, toys, games, drugs, gambling and the internet all give opportunities to achieve this "ignorance is bliss" status.

The self analysis of whether to concern ourselves with these problems is an examination of our conscience. It is typically avoided by a majority of society. It may not be purposely avoided but it ranks low for most people and is low on list of "things to do". There are so many more interesting and easier options available to fill the 24 hours we all have each day. It is the "getting around to it" (like the wooden token with the word TUIT written on it.....getting a round TUIT). Most people never pick their TUIT up or never really look for one in the first place.

The conclusion indicates if the integrity, we avoid thinking about, were to be more closely associated, taught and exhibited the problems facing society would be self correcting. If we all clean our own door step the whole world would be clean.

### 11.4 Prison Reform

The existence of prisons is another symptom of the problems resulting from a lack of integrity. These institutions are filled with individuals who did not think they would be caught committing that particular crime for which they were convicted. The cause for committing that crime may have resulted from involuntary responses to more deeply seated problems like poverty or addiction but the fact remains they are now in prison and their numbers continues to grow. The explanation for why the problems of poverty and addiction are related was already addressed, so it is now down to answering which comes first, the chicken or the egg?

The incentive for reforming the prison system makes it difficult to entice any bureaucracy to be involved. The problem must be addressed honestly. There are numerous communities around the United States whose very existence depends on a constant flow of new inmates into the penal system to thrive.

The mantra of "law and order" is very popular with no one wanting those committing crimes interspersed in our society. The need for law and order is primal and part of security necessary for a functioning society. But when they are at cross purposes regarding ways to address the problem, it is because they are addressing the symptom and not the problem. Crime, prisons and lawlessness, in general are all a result of the integrity issue to which we continually return.

The need to perfect the question when addressing each of these issues is hopefully being understood and internalized by now. Again, to solve any problem, the problem must be exactly defined or perfected and certain the issue is not symptomatic of the underlying concern.

### 11.5 Racism or any Discrimination

The definition of racism or any other "ism" is fundamentally rooted in the violation of fairness, honesty, sustainability and integrity. The ironic part of the movements surrounding this issue: the ones who points it out seem to be the guiltiest of the very discrimination for which they are condemning.

The hypocrisy is in the propaganda behind the word "Diversity". Their claim is diversity is a great "gift" to society. But these groups resist any encouragement to assimilate. The gift the liberal agenda seems to be interested in promoting is only the charm of their customs and traditions and not in making them American citizens who want to integrate into our systems which made this country great. Where the real gift lies is not readily apparent if it exists in the first place?

The liberal agenda's approach is to make various nationalities victims. The term racist is used to describe anyone who impugns or limits the practice of someone else's traditions, regardless of how contrary that tradition is or in spite of it being against this country's laws. The old saying "When in France, do as the French" seems to have no bearing or influence on foreigners being polite or gracious, as guests in this country.

The other issue around diversity, where integrity is lacking, is when they have a "collection of people" that includes every color, sex, age or nationality in the mix. The objective being promoted is only appearance. The hypocrisy is anyone in the group looks different but they all have identical political positions. The cynical observation is colleges today have become a place with everyone looks different but everyone thinks the same way. The integrity issue is further compromised when their disingenuous mantra is: inclusiveness is always good if we agree with your point of view.

When I was growing up in Nebraska, we were oblivious to the poverty status we were given, until we were told we were poor later in life. The same with racism or the political correct derivative called "diversification". Children are not aware of these differences until they are taught. They are indoctrinated about the differences and then taught to exploit those differences. They are trained to find ways to "game the system" for restitution or to identify a villain to blame for their situation.

The act of discrimination is an integrity issue that propagates movements, riots, bureaucracies and stereotypes that spawn entire industries. These entities often seem to have no desire or are unaware of the real problem they are trying to solve. But their objective is to continually propagate more discrimination to keep the funding and expand the careers of bureaucrats. If the discrimination problem went away the bureaucracy would stop funding it.

The celebrations and organizations that evolve around a class or group are calling attention to discrimination of any and all types. They range from NAACP, Black Congressional Caucus, Black Lives Matter, ACORN and Black History Month, International Women's Day, LGBT History Month, Southern Poverty Law Center or National Organization for Women with the list expanding to identifying any possible different in appearance or belief system. This is blatantly discriminatory. The aspect of the first black president seemed only to make the entire matter worse. There are more attempts now at continuing the awareness than ever before, with the issue never seeming to improve.

The reason for the lack of progress on discrimination issues, along with all the other issues listed previously, is simply a lack of integrity. We do not seem to individually recognize the dishonestly of individual convictions that prevents us from confronting this inconsistency in fairness. This occurs either through intimidation or political correctness that has infected the entire society.

**11.6 Transgender Issues**

The amazing part of society and life is each of us are individuals with a free will. It is hard to fathom that every one of the seven billion people on this planet is different, but they are and they must be accepted for who they are. They are to be accepted not for any dysfunctional behavior but for the expectation that if they have any differences, they live by the "Golden Rule"[45]. The transgender issues have nearly the exact complexities as that of racism. The population size[48] is the only difference. This difference between the sexes, regardless of the variation, is the only real way a society or any species of plant or animal can survive and procreate. The temptation to classify or group species into a phylum, class or kingdom is the scientific approach of a biologist. But when these classifications exploit superficial differences for victimization purposes is where the lack of integrity becomes an issue.

The fundamental position of evolution, that society adapted over the millennia, that delivered us to this point is the recognition of the individual sexes. This was designed to protect the family unit for the sustainability of our society. The recognition of same sex relationships by giving them privileges reserved to married couples is discriminatory to all the single people of the world. To re-characterize this institution is the result of political correctness, where responsibility is no longer a requirement, while living their life. The desire to encourage this diversity, while exploiting that difference, is denying rights to an entire group of single people who accept the responsibility of their own role in life. Any exception that excludes other single individuals is simply not fair.

The expectation of receiving special or different treatment because that difference, is not a reason to discriminate. It is ripe for inspiring conflict. Expecting a solution where past discrimination cases require restitution is like the "son being punished for the sins of the father" and has no basis in logic and quickly extrapolates into the ridiculous.

The attempts at exacerbating these differences completely compromises any semblance of integrity. It is nearly impossible to rationalize this as fair, honest or sustainable with the fairness question: "would you accept the solution proposed, if the tables were turned?" Almost without exception, this attempt at exacting revenge for past grievances, where traditional values are now found to be discriminatory, rings hollow with none of the core values expressed earlier being respected or observed.

No one can tell anyone how to live but to shy away from any responsibility because of the decision they made to live that way, is hypocritical. They may think they have feelings for a given tendency, and we all have various feelings of various tendencies. But when integrity is present, the expectation of completely overturning traditional conventions to accommodate them is unfair and selfish.

We all have a cross to bear in life. But the secret in life, in bearing that cross, is not what happens to us but how we deal with what happens to us. The platitude of "what doesn't kill you always makes you stronger" seems to apply.

There is a story of the young teenager found praying to God, with unrelenting requests to be given a lighter cross to bear in life. God, finally hearing the prayer of the teenage said: "I will give you an opportunity to trade in your cross for another." Upon hearing this, the teenager was delighted and was shown a room filled with crosses of all shapes, sizes and weight. After thoroughly looking around, the teenager finally made a decision and chose a small cross that was no larger than two tooth picks glued together. God took the cross and looked at it and asked "Is this the cross you want?" The teenager answered "yes". God turned over the small cross, only to inform the teenager: "This *IS* your cross!"

# Chapter 12

# Politicians think they are Leaders?

The concept of how the United States is managed and directed is being propagandized by using two words that disguise their true objective. These two words are "leader" and "democracy".

Our Great Country is often wrongly mischaracterized, by the media and many people who talk about our government, as being a Democracy[83]. The proof of this misunderstanding comes when the question: How long has the United States of America been a democracy? The typical answer is: from 1789 when the constitution was adopted by a majority of the 13 Colonies. The truth is the constitution does not make this country a democracy. The adoption of The Constitution makes a set of laws and principles, with the bill of rights, that give us a Republic[84]. This is not like a democracy and it is important to understand the difference.

Ben Franklin said: "if we give the citizens of this country a pure democracy, they would vote the country into bankruptcy in two generations." To not realize this is an insult to logic and the human condition. The lack of integrity along with selfish motives, that are not sustainable, would quickly ruin the country.

The best example of how dangerous a pure democracy is: If a group gathers and a majority voted to take your car, the democratic process would cause this self appointed group to now own your car. This is blatantly unfair and no hardworking citizen who bought that car would tolerate it being confiscated.

The real atrocity happens when the voters then sell or part out the car and divide the money among those who voted to "steal the car" in the first place. This is a form of socialism. Again, a very disturbing scenario of what happens in a democracy. For this to happen requires a complete lack of accepting any of the core values of which we speak, especially integrity.

By closely analyzing the results of a democracy, aside from the extreme case mentioned above, it is assumed that everyone is supposed to have a say in the outcome. The number of individual opinions in any group is usually only slightly less than the number of individuals. Because of this distribution of opinions on ways to solving any problem, they democratically select solutions that will never be the extremes. It will never be the best nor will it be the worst. It will be the perfect normal or medium. It is be the very center or average or, put another way, perfectly mediocre.

The function of the Republic is: To protect the individual from the masses or "mob rule". Laws written with a sense of fairness where the whim of taking someone's car arbitrarily would not be allowed

With our democratically selected congress, the theory is this system provides elected individuals to manage the government. Their life experience gets them elected. This experience caused this, slightly above the average individual, to gain the votes and confidence of the people. This vetting process, known as the election, forces these individuals to survive the "trial by fire" call a campaign. It should show something about the character of the individual going through the process. The system requires an above average skill set to survive, much less win.

The second insult to our intelligence is use of the word "leader" to describe our politicians. This is also false. The president of this country is not the leader, he is the CEO or top manager for the business of running the country. That function is to implement the things that are fair, honest, sustainable with integrity and stop any attempt to do things that violate these core values. The job also requires working within the framework of the constitution and not to "reinvent the wheel", a tendency of a more liberal agenda.

The talents to "live" these core values should be exemplified by our so call managers or politicians. Our country is not headed by leaders but by people who call themselves politicians, hired to manage. A country with a leader is a country with a dictator. Those leaders (dictators) tell everyone what to do and when. In the United States our politicians are not leaders, but "managers".  They manage the country's systems, like a business, according to a document called The Constitution.  The leaders of The United States of America are: "We The People".  This means that our national "managers" will never be much better than us.  If we, as citizens, do not have Integrity or expect true integrity to be a part of our society, it is not logical to expect our national managers have it, either.

The self declared leaders of the world have names like Adolph Hitler, Saddam Hussein, Kim Jong-un or Bashar al-Assad.  They are supreme dictators who command their citizens who have little or no ability or opportunity to participate in the process.  Their personal interests, as dictator, are primary in their role with their survival the only thing that matters.  They often describe their leadership as the will of the people but this disguise is "thin" with everyone knowing it is a complete lie and too afraid to express their opinion.  The lack of integrity in making such a statement speaks volumes about their objective, as dictators, and their method of managing a country.  It is not close to any business model but a demonstration of "might and wealth is right" with their whims the law of the land.

The leader of the United States of America is stated in the first seven words of the preamble: "We the People of the United States".  We hire (elect) managers to run this country according The Constitution.  That document provides the framework to do the three basic things we want our government to manage:

1. Provide Security
2. Provide Infrastructure
3. Provide Laws to promote domestic tranquility

We are not a democracy but a "democratic republic" where "We, The People", select the managers.  The expectation is: these managers have our core values of Honesty, Fairness, Integrity and will do that which is Sustainable and not bankrupt the country.

Democracy is simply mob rule. We can see this by demonstrations that turn violent and destructive. If a group of your friends decides to vote and take your car, that is democracy. A mob can decide to throw out any consideration of fairness or honesty. A mob is a group acting in unison. It becomes unpredictable and very dangerous dictatorship where all the core values are ignored or propagandized as not fair. If they decide the "management class", with their ancestors, are thought to be repressive or somehow responsible for all the atrocities that occurred over history, they will try to seek revenge. It is the liberal way of justifying a way of exacting restitution and compensation from that management class, always to the benefit and unfair enrichment of the demonstrators.

A Democracy is a way of destroying the individual rights for everyone. The result of a democracy is mob rule with the only possible outcome, a dictatorship in the limit. The dictatorial process will unilaterally decide things when the inability of finding acceptable solutions, becomes impossible or intolerable if it were to continue.

A Republic is a way of preserving individual rights. The result of a republic is respectful consideration of all participants in the fact that "what goes around comes around". The fair administration of justice and benefits are practically guaranteed by the system. The eventual outcome is a manager who controls the situation to keep it from becoming mob rule.

When radical segments believe we have a democracy and demand things must be changed, is where mob rule starts. Just because the majority want it does not permit "the kids to run the school" or the "prisoners should guard the Jail". The problem is there are no responsible entities to manage, maintain or fund the system. This is what happens when there is a political coup. There is no logical organization to manage the country. It is not practical or sustainable.

Democracy is one step away from a socialistic system, with a dictator. The dictator will eventually assume power over those who refuse to take care of themselves, forcing those trying to care for themselves to pay the expenses of those who want to be "baby sat".

The entire democracy paradigm is unsustainable and will function only with a lot of bureaucratic red tape and rules. This practically guarantees that nothing will get accomplished while wasting a lot of money trying.

The epitome of hypocrisy is the example when the Democrat Party originally wanted to call themselves the Socialist Party, but they changed the name to Democrat to eliminate the bad associations with socialism.

This is another example of the many discussions showing how the lack of integrity is the foundation of all the problems listed in the introduction.

# Chapter 13

## Not Knowing Your Purpose in Life

The universal questions in life are:

1. What is the purpose of life?
2. What is the true meaning of Success?
3. Is there a life after death?
4. Is there a God?

All of these questions have been debated for several millennia. Some will say the answers are not important if we have "faith". This is true if our curiosity does not cause us to hunger for more understanding of the marvelous universe of which we are all a part.

We should now be able to address the first two questions. It is important to be remember the answer to this first pair of questions includes this understanding: It is not the destination we are seeking but to know the process we must experience during our entire physical existence.

These first two fundamental questions have answers! The test is to determine if they are the truest answers. That answer comes in the form of the scientific approach used in answering any question. A theorem in mathematics or geometry is: a statement made that has never been proven wrong. The answers derived from using these theories are considered the most correct, to that point.

Applying these principle to the questions "What is the Purpose of Life?" or the "Meaning of Success?" one must be brutally objective and subscribe to the theorem's definition. With this approach the answers we find would seem to be the best answer available. The system used to find answers to these two questions will give insights to answers for other questions about life. The questions can then be addressed with more confidence. A sound decision making approach gives objectiveness and assurance the answer will be more usable and carry more validity with logical and a less emotional foundation.

The true purpose for our existence is simpler than we would expect when considering the ultimate fate each of us must face. The only result we can all expect is that we will die. With that fact established, the only variable remaining is how much time we have remaining between this moment and when we take our final breath. Since that time is not known to anyone, the only sensible response in addressing our individual purpose is: do not waste the finite amount of time we have.

We should NOT purposely waste time. To know if we are wasting time we should define what is "a waste" of time. Time can not be saved. We all have only 24 hours a day. The only remaining activity is to do only those things that are not a waste. With this mindset, the result should spawn traits found in true leaders.

True leaders are not dictators. True leaders display their leadership by example, only! That example must include the awareness of doing productive things, all in an effort to make the world a better place. That better place may be as simple as "not leaving a mess" for others to clean up when we are gone. If we are not trying to make the world a better place, we are truly wasting the limited time we have.

This is the definition for the purpose of life: **"Making the world a better place"** and saving our soul in the process. The greatest compliment we can give to anyone is to imitate their actions and activities. Activities without a method or system, that no one would want to imitate, is telling and not a good sign. To make the world a better place means making and teaching the methods and procedures that helped you be successful. The definition of success is to "be and teach" how to be self sufficient. To be able to teach and show, how to negotiate things through all the situations that occur in life, is success. It is simply standard problem solving by perfecting the question.

There is an answer to every question if the question is perfected and if the agenda is fully defined. If this were not true, the very existence of a computer would not be possible. If the programming of the computer addresses all the rules and accepted truths, there can be only one correct answer to any question.

We see question/answer "face offs" when the media is asking politicians or authority figures how they are planning to address an issue or problem. The reason for these question and answer forums are usually in response to an unforeseen event or disaster. The little game of cat and mouse that happens at these impromptu events is to position the media, not to promoter the guise of free speech and transparency but an attempt to control the outcome by "trapping" the politician in an inconsistency.

Any situation, no matter how innocent, that appears inconsistent with integrity gives the media an opening to ask questions to explain that inconsistency. This point was made when Vice President Pence stated that he would never have a meal in public without his wife present. If he did violate his own rules and was ever asked about it, no matter what the response, there is no way of winning in the court of public opinion. The conclusion is to never compromise one's integrity or do anything to make it seem plausible for compromise, regardless of whether anyone will notice.

I experienced the "gauntlet" of a political campaign where these media duels are laced with hypocrisy and dishonest agendas designed to entrap and embarrass. The media is not interested in finding any constructive information or action plans to improve any situation. Instead, they are always looking for a sound bite to show inconsistencies.

The disappointing part is: if a "perfect", fully detailed response was given, the media would probably not be interested or understand it and when reported, it would be condensed into a quick sound bite. This is done to either sensationalize the story or use it as an opportunity to impugn. This is the main reason President Trump tweets. There is no chance for the media to re-characterize the statement, except in the minds of those wanting to use it to advance an alternative agenda.

In our age of technology, this game is being gradually exposed. There are numerous news sources and social media opportunities with very "different takes" on the same issue come up. These contradicting impressions are being seen as inconsistent. These inconsistencies unmask the self serving or less than honest agenda of the reporter. Today, the other side of the story is difficult to hide and impossible to censor, as was done when there were only few sources for news in the middle of the twentieth century. They all carried the same story with the same spin.

Today, the cycle of these "little games" of "tit for tat", with the news cycle constantly becoming shorter, is impossible to always escape unscaved. As cycle time accelerates the ability to connect the dots regarding the exposure of these dishonest agendas, happens almost instantly. They will continue to happen at ever faster rates going forward. The good thing about this is the speed of this cycle will cause the "media game" to be less affective in their ability to spread propaganda. The exposure of any fake news, will be minimized with the media unable to respond quickly by recharacterizing any story in this age of tweeting or instant messaging. This is good news and an opportunity to naturally improve integrity in this age of technological.

The ability to force the questioner to "perfect the initial question", will further short circuit this propaganda cycle. It will go a long way in reducing or eliminating the possibility of giving the media any opportunity to advance a particular agenda. This lack of fundamental integrity along with their desire to still appear relevant in the news cycle is causing concern by media and the politicians they support. To address this, the use of third party "filters" called "fact checkers" is proposed by the media to give the appearance of validity.

These third party systems are to ascertain the accuracy or relevance of news, but there are dangerous and unintended consequences here as well. The credibility of the fact checker is now suspected giving us the return of propaganda under a different name. The desire to eliminate propaganda, only resulted in a thicker layer of "fake news".

It has come to the point where Wikipedia[65] has been known, while in their process of perfecting their answers, to refuse the contributing content of the author of the very book they are reviewing. They considered it not credible because of the overwhelming influence paid consultants and bots[67], who monitor Wikipedia, have upon any content that contradict their propaganda on that subject. This sort of pirating of Wikipedia content exacerbates the problem. It has become a cottage industry, growing with the advent of programs where these bot algorithms create massive numbers of re-tweets making "fake news" appear entirely credible in spite of having no basis in fact.

The First Amendment's right of free speech is in the cross hairs. This phenomenon, with the censorship of accurate content, stops accurate content by using consensus, not facts. The result is the dishonest agenda wins. These are all classic examples of "astroturfing"[66] is the epitome of a lack of integrity that has become more pervasive in the world.

Again, the integrity issue surfaces as the cause of these problems. If the trust and honest altruistic values were more prevalent in the hearts of those in authority, where laws are instigated to only address the symptom, this "arms race" mentality would not happen.

To approach any Q+A situation in this fashion would greatly improve the opportunity to infuse more integrity into the process. The integrity issue requires the awareness of truth, honesty and sustainability in everything that is said or done. The temptation to deflect, shield or sidestep these core values requires the ultimate in integrity and is difficult do consistently. But if we can make it easier to notice those points, by maintaining these core values, integrity would happen more naturally and make the world a considerably better place.

The adage that says: "if someone can, someone will try" is the human condition that has strong evolutionary traits in our society. The only way to overcome this condition is to require the human condition to gradually evolve to a place where this temptation "to do something that is not honest" is not rewarded or made profitable.

With the technological advances of faster computers and ever larger data bases, the subjective solution to any problem would gradually become extinct. Since the human condition is always involved, eliminating the consternation and pain of this trial and error approach is nearly impossible to stop. It is contrary to our genetic makeup.

If answers come too easily, they are not appreciated. The mantra: "easy come, easy go" is another human condition that will be very difficult to "bred out" of our human condition.

But, if the ingredient of integrity were not such a rare and fleeting commodity, society would be a place where the list of problems and concerns would be considerably shorter. This would leave us only with problems caused by natural disasters. We would no longer have the problems that result from the human condition where there is no integrity or trust between fellow humans.

Problem solving has now moved to the next evolutionary step because of the introduction of technology. When temptation of giving in to our individual emotions in the problem solving is eliminated, the result will be answers that are objective with little, if any, dishonest answers that violate the four core values

IF the objective problem solving approach is accepted, the extrapolation of this process gives rise to the concept of crowd sourcing. A recent PBS[71] special "The Crowd and The Cloud" demonstrated the ways older and retired individuals can be assimilated with the use of their computers to address everything from mapping remote parts of the planet to tracing brain synapse[72] connections of brain scans. The amount of work for paid researchers would take three decades and billions of dollars. But when compared to the thousands volunteers, who want to contribute, it could be done it in a couple of weeks for free.

The term crowd sourcing is simply the concept of having everyone with a computer able to contribute in some small way. Crowd sourcing, in the technological world, is simply known as "The Cloud"[70].

The power of The Watson Computer is contained in the fact that all the information in the world is being used in finding the solution to any problem. This "cloud" concept is a two way street. It not only contains all the information in the world, it also contains all the opinions of all those in the world with access to it. This means the integrity of the entire system is directly related to the average integrity of all who participate in the process.

The problem of lacking integrity seems to be a direct function to the amount of enrichment gained by the cheater. If the incentive is to have an individual doing something with their time, in order to make the world a better place, this would be an ideal application of their brain power. They simply want to make some use of their time and have nothing to gain or lose by cheating. This is the ideal situation where cloud knowledge and problem solving could be used.

With this, it is now becoming possible to assimilate and use this massive resource of the individual human brain in a collective manner. There are ways available to assemble, with the use of the cloud, this brain power to work as a single organism to address massive programming tasks that were previously were impossible to tackle, for no other reason than the human resource cost of doing these tasks.

This is where the "I" in integrity becomes ever more important and vital in making the world a better place. Integrity is impossible to police. A lack of integrity is not a crime that is punishable. It is a part of "saving your soul", but that judgment is not available for publication during our life time. It is simply something that must be valued, lived, internalized and shown during our entire life. It is contagious, just like a lack of integrity is contagious, as well. If watching someone doing things that seem to be helpful by others, they may be likely to do the same thing.

There is a saying: "Dysfunctionality is perfectly obvious in everyone else but ourselves." It is impossible not to notice all the idiosyncrasies that irritate others as well. It is also nearly impossible have an idiosyncrasy be universally despised, because there are those in the world with that same idiosyncrasy that will accept it. The old adage "misery loves company" applies as people like to be around people who like doing the same things. If integrity was found to be attractive in a larger part of society, the world would definitely become a better place.

The objective we all need to address is for the world to have integrity. It is to do our individual part of keeping the world clean by first cleaning our own doorstep. If everyone did, the problem would be solved. Since we can only make our self do anything, all we can do is try by setting the example.

In Chapter 4 we made reference to "Click and Clack the Tappet Brothers" and their observation of whether information increases or decreases when two idiots are conferring. This sets up an example of self examination that has a similar mantra regarding integrity. If you are conferring with someone over a moral dilemma, would the total amount of integrity between the two of you increase or decrease?

# Chapter 14

## The Real Purpose for Prayer

I was raised in a very devout Catholic family with a saint for a mother and the most honest man I have ever known for a father. The debate of how our parents influence the lives of their children is classic and has been a part of psychological discussions for centuries. The question of whether our behavior is "nurtured" or "natured" will continue to be studied with the conclusion of little value if it is ever settled.

Whether our behavior is determined by how we were are raised or by the evolution of our blood line, it does not change the fact that we are all individually responsible for our own actions and have a free will to do what ever we desire. There are no excuses for attitudes that cause destructive activity because of what happened to our great-great grandfather by some other blood line that wronged them. The need to be fair, honest and act sustainably is fundamental and basic with our individual integrity the only thing that influences which road we each take.

The old Chinese saying: "If everyone would keep their own door step clean, the whole world would be clean." is true. If all of us had good integrity, all the problems in the world would be solved. The golden rule would be standard procedure, there would be no reason for door locks, police or prisons where everyone there was caught doing something they thought they would not be caught doing.

How is praying involved in this dialogue? It may not be perfectly obvious, but we all have free will. We can individually act in any way we are physically or intellectually capable of maneuvering. We can try to violate the laws of physics but the consequences of jumping off a building, expecting to fly, will usually meet with a sudden stop when you hit the ground with a thud.

The belief in a God or any other supreme being has also been a large part of human society for a dozen millennia. This is not a discussion to prove the existence of a God but the clarification of what we can expect as a result if all of us have a free will.

The list of core values: honesty, fairness, sustainability and integrity are supposed to be consistent in all laws from the Ten Commandments to the Rotary Four Way Test[16] as well as the Golden Rule and other world religions. It is the basis of Natural Law[17] as well as the rules and customs found in the earliest recorded writings of ancient civilizations and their religious beliefs. They are all rooted in the need to trust and be trustworthy. These values are also consistent with how we deal with our God or our self if one is agnostic.

With the establishment of a God, there is a human tendency to want to talk to "Him". There is a romantic concept of having a personal and loving dialogue with God along with the expectation of peace and harmony resulting from those "conversations". We will call these conversations, prayer and even agnostics revert to prayer, just in case, if not some sort of wishful thinking.

Churches continue to encourage these "conversations with God" as a way of easing the stress of daily life and the problems life brings upon us. We all have a cross to bear as there is always the force of gravity that causes each of us to exert energy to overcome it. This energy only comes from the food we eat so we can receive the energy required to work and make a living, etc. etc. etc.

The point that we pray to God has evolved to a point where we expect God to intercede or do things for us.

These prayers are said so God will fix this, or make that happen or cause something to go away or improve something else. The prayers become requests for God to intercede in our life in some way, making things easier.

The problem with this sort of prayer is they start to sound like begging. They are prayers of intercession. They are asking God to do something for us so we do not have work as hard or ask God violate the laws of physics to make something easier is some way. This is NOT how God works. If he did operate in that fashion, we would not have a truly "Free Will". To expect God to function in this way is lazy and irresponsible. God helps those who help themselves and he expects us to do his will. Although this is not a biblical quote, it is no less true. He wills each of us to make the world a better place and save our soul by setting a good example by being honest, fair with integrity and not to waste those gifts, resources and talents he gave each of us. We pray in adoration and appreciation for this world and our abilities to make it a better place. Prayer is not begging. It is the thanksgiving and appreciation that we have some understanding of a world we live in, while trying to save our soul.

I have heard the argument, in an attempt to show that prayers of intercession exist by quoting the "Lord's Prayer" or the "Our Father". The part that says "give us this day our daily bread" is NOT an intercession for food. It is in the context of thanking God for our "Free Will", the daily gift of being able to live with "free will" and our decision to, hopefully, do his will. The proof of this concept comes in the next phrase "and forgive us our trespasses". There is no obvious relationship between "bread and trespasses" so the only logical purpose for these two phrases to be said in sequence is to show the contrast. If we use our free will to do wrong, we must acknowledge it and request forgiveness for making the mistake.

My mother would gather us around to pray the rosary every evening. As a child we didn't question it. But as we grew older and there were more interesting activities available, like television. It was difficult to refrain from acting out and complaining. As I became older and able to better express myself, I asked her "Why do we pray?" The standard answer was something along the line of "that we all get along" or "that we all stay healthy", "that we stay safe" or the most common one in the 1950's when there were numerous draughts we "prayed for rain".

It wasn't until I was in high school in conversations with my grandfather, when more in depth discussions of religion and world politics became more interesting, I realize some inconsistencies in my mother's reason for praying. If we had free will, praying God would "do something" for us was not part of the deal. Our prayer needed to be only in appreciation for the gifts we were given and in thanksgiving for the ability to use those gifts to make the world a better place.

Prayer is a form of problem solving. Earlier in Chapter 2 we discussed perfecting the question. This is the process of exactly defining the problem, where the answer would simply "fall out" when the question was turned into a statement.

Prayer is a form of problem solving. We do not pray for rain but we thank God for the ability to figure out what to do "if it doesn't rain". Not everyone will go broke if it doesn't rain. There are those who will survive. They are the ones who prayed and in that conversation with God, about the problem and figured out what to do. They were perfecting the question to a point where it was solved, with out rain.

My main purpose for this written effort is to help others realize how to make the world a little better place for those who will come after us. I trust my insights and explanations of the world's problems help in understanding the causes of those problems and the fact they are caused by the lack of a single ingredient: the lack of integrity.

I trust this book will motivate those who read it to realize your influence in solving the problems of the world is far greater than we are lead to believe. This concept can be infectious if we have the courage to expose these ideas through our example and actions. They are not difficult to understand nor are they hard to implement if the incentive for this behavior is encouraged by society. Currently it is considerably easier and more profitable to act is a way that is contrary these principle. We can only try to advance the incentive to have "good integrity".

Giving up and resigning ourselves to do nothing is not constructive and must be discouraged through our personal example and accept the fact that political correctness is no excuse. We must continue to make every effort to encourage integrity.......

# Epilogue

The premise of this book was to logically deduce that all our "so called" problems in the world are actually only the symptoms. The real problem is a simple lack of integrity that results in all the world's problems. The real irony of this conclusion is all these symptoms are easily solved by society when everyone can be trusted.

"Those who don't study history are doomed to repeat it. Yet those who *do* study history are doomed to stand by helplessly while everyone else repeats it."

If a lack of trust exists, all bets are off and society will revert to a state of increasing entropy,[91] that state of matter when everything moves toward a more random position. We can not violate the laws of physics. The only way to reverse entropy (achieve more order) is by adding energy. That energy must come from each of us in society. If members of society refuse to make the world a better place, the result is more randomness, chaos and dysfunctionality, not to mention more work for everyone else. These acts of omission are the result of a lack of integrity giving us the situation we have in the world.

History proves this by a hoax propagated upon society, mainly by history majors who try to justify their degree. It is the mantra: "History must be studied so we don't repeat it." This is an excellent example of unconscious incompetence. History is replete with stories of mistakes, bad decisions and flawed logic by bureaucrats and politicians who were too stupid to know better or simply lacked integrity.

History, like the news, is only interesting if it is weird, dysfunctional, a crime or an accident. Those things that are out of the ordinary. Studying all the wrong answers and the mistakes made over time is ridiculous and a perfect example of insanity....doing the same thing over and over expecting a different result. When engineering students leave engineering to become history majors, the common observation was the GPA of both departments goes up.

No problem has ever been solved by insisting on the endless study of "what did not work". This is why government fail to solve problems. This is why problem solving methods used by businesses, scientist and engineers only extrapolate from a position of the last best results and only put energy into that which gives a better result. The form of that result should have been defined at the start of the problems solving exercise and was covered in Chapter 2. When these steps are skipped, it is no wonder the world finds itself in the current situation.

The lack of integrity is the biggest problem in the world and without it no one can be trusted. There seems to be no incentive for anyone to aspire to have true integrity. It has been shown consistently, it is considerably more profitable to cheat, thinking they can avoid the consequences of being caught for their actions and decisions. Courts and politicians seem to consistently move toward a state of increasing entropy (more randomness) by becoming more politically correct.

I stated in the beginning of this book, it is not a religious work and I am not making a commercial to recruit or discourage membership to any particular religion. I was born and raised Catholic and try to practice my religion as faithfully as I can. By applying some of the principles of my first book and studying the church with the concepts in that book, once the reverence of the religion is filtered out, there are brilliant reasons for what the Catholic Church does.

The lack of trust or integrity is the world's greatest problem. Also, it is impossible to force integrity upon anyone. The path of least resistance has shown it is easier and more profitable to cheat than to operate with integrity. There must be incentive to have integrity, if we expect others to contribute to making the world a better place.

There are only few models in the real world where the incentive to strive for greater integrity exists, namely the United States Marines and the Boy Scouts. The incentive in these examples is the privilege of "Staying in the Club" or not losing privileges if caught violating the rules.

In the Marines that discouragement is a dishonorable discharge which impacts the rest of their life, not to mention the feeling of resentment felt when other soldiers would refuse to pick those violators to "watch their back" in combat situation.

In the Boy Scouts, it can be as simple as losing the privilege to start of fire or carry a knife, if a higher ranking scout catches them cheating or violating any rule. These are big deals to a ten year boy who wants to participate.

Both these examples work on the "negative incentive" principle to do the right things. This is an example of the means justifying the end with true honest integrity still missing because there would be no punishment if they were not caught.

I confess I am not the best practicing Catholic, but in the deeper study of why The Catholic Church does what it , is pure genius and unique to The Catholic Church for the following three reasons with explanations:

1. **The Church is the only religion that practices the sacrament of penance that Catholics call "going to confession".**

In the business world, information is everything. The desire to know the game plan of your competitor is the most sought after and useful information. It is the only item that can not be found in books. It can only be extrapolated by the study of known previous thoughts and action patterns by that competitor. No one studies what they did wrong with the expectation of having that competitor repeat that mistake. They would expect their competitor to be logical, particularly if you feel there is no apparent advantage between you and the competitor is taking some of your business. (If the competitor is an idiot and you are losing little business, don't waste your time).

The best way to receive information is to have those involved in operation tell you honestly, with all the rules of fair play expected to be followed after the information is learned. The rule: "if you live by the sword you will die by the sword" applies. If one wins by cheating, you will eventually be caught cheating.

Working for 30 years in the corporate world, the aspect of trust and openness is the greatest commodity of any business organization. If I were running an organization, knowing the inter-most feelings of those who trusted me with that information is the ultimate compliment.

Creating this situation in the real world is impossible, but that is exactly what The Catholic Church does as a standard procedure.

When a pastor comes to a parish, what better way to know how to deal with the personalities and problems of any group, than have them tell you their problems, concerns, dysfunctionalities, and sins, anonymously. The need for knowing the individual is really not useful. But the fact there are things that fit into patterns would be enormously useful in learning how to manage a parish or any collection of people who have a singular goal, but have bad habits.

**2. The Church is not subject to political correctness nor should it succumb to pressures of modernity.**

The approach of using confession to advance an honest and sincere effort to make the world a better place is nearly perfect in its applications by The Church. There is no need for propaganda or coercive attempts at manipulation of the parishioners through disingenuous agendas from politically correct movements.

It is honest, simple, sincere and extremely effective with little energy needed to perpetuate the method. It has all the ingredients found in the four core values of honesty, fairness, sustainability and integrity.

The need for a church to be a "drum major" by standing in front of a parade so they can call themselves leaders is eliminated. The system *IS* the leader with the results a nearly perpetual system that actually self corrects.

This correction mechanism is when integrity is present in the entire process where it is assumed, lived and demonstrated by all parties. This is a very appealing and comforting.

**3. The Church built a self correcting mechanism into its teaching that makes the true practicing Catholic want to strive for greater integrity.**

In the act of confession, the belief that one's sins are truly forgiven after fulfilling the penance given by the priest, is also self correcting. To go to confession in the first place is a monumental task for many Catholics and the state of mind of the penitent must be free of hypocrisy.

For one to expect to be completely forgiven for any indiscretion, sin or malicious act would be impossible if they were not truly sorry for their actions. This leads to the aspect of human nature where these "sins" are difficult to avoid and often repeated. But, in the act of confession the belief that God understands that we will continually succumb to these temptation, would ring hollow if that sin is continually re-confessed.

The very act of realizing our own hypocrisy when this happens, make it embarrassing to your inner self if this happen too often. This very realization, to any self respecting adult, should be discomforting and be the incentive to be exactly what you want the world to think you are.

Like the Chinese saying: "The world would be completely clean if everyone cleaned their own doorstep" applies perfectly. It is the only remaining action item for each of us for the remainder of our lives.

If we all understand and teach these principles by exhibiting honesty, fairness and integrity, all the world's problems would go away. This is may be impossible, but we should never stop trying.

# THE COVER AND TITLE

The Mobius strip[47] and The Klein Bottle[46] are ideal examples and a perfect analogy for the word integrity. With the strip, one can never be sure if one is touching the inside or outside of the paper strip as with the bottle where the outside of the container is inside of the bottle and difficult to know exactly when the sides change.

Integrity, like the Mobius strip or the Klein bottle, is where one's insides are not hidden and fully exposed with the inside and the outside appearing without any change or physical conversion. Integrity is the state of being when ones true emotions and convictions are not hidden but openly shown, naturally and constantly, without embarrassment or fear of undesirable social reactions.

Integrity is the deepest and most personal of all our emotions, with only you knowing for sure what you are feeling, thinking or planning. Your words and actions only hint at knowing what is going on inside of you. Those around you can only sense a perception of who you are and it is not possible to absolutely prove that to anyone. The closest indication is the consistency of ones actions through all situations that people observe about you. We must continually project and protect our integrity if we truly value what it represents. It takes only one inconsistency or a display to the contrary, to completely undermine the impression of your true integrity.

A lack of integrity is the only sin that is continual and not situational. All other sins are ones of commission, usually requiring a specific action at some point in time to make it a sin. The lack of integrity is the continual living of a lie.

Integrity is who you are and it can't be instantly switched "on" or "off". If someone can make such an instantaneous switch in demeanor, that is known as a psychopaths, and they are dangerous people with whom to associate.

Of course, this all refers to good integrity. As mentioned in Chapter One, Hitler had integrity. He had the ultimate in bad integrity. He was not the least bit hesitant to fully and completely express his innermost feelings and distain for those he blamed for the repression of Germany after WW I. It comes down to determining which is the better of two evils from which to select. Like Frank Lloyd Wright asked: "Is it better to have sincere conceit or fake humility?" Base on the premise of this book, sincerity is always better because deception and mistrust is the root of all the problems in the world.

The depth of integrity comes with maturation when one has a heightened sense of self awareness. It, theoretically, comes when we see obvious signs of hypocrisy in people who are unaware of the transparency they unconsciously project. The virtue called "integrity" is not a group sport nor is it something we are born with. There is the point where the innocence of youth is transformed, as we grow and learn through observation of good examples. Integrity should permeate from the first leaders we meet in our young lives, our parents, and hopefully become something we can emulate. It is difficult to teach integrity without gaining it through these observations.

The United States education system tries to teach integrity by trying to describe it and not demonstrating it. Integrity is not something that can be announced or declared. It must be demonstrated, by all our educators, politicians and business leaders to have any believability or credibility. The general consensus of what is being actually taught in schools today does not speak well of today's education system based on the behaviors exhibited by the products being produced by these institutions. Integrity must be internalized though continual observations and not through indoctrination. It is the most individualistic of all the "Core Values". It is the kernel that eventually sprouts into all the other "Core Values".

The "I" in the title is "you" and our obligation to have integrity "infect" everyone with whom YOU associate, by example. Integrity is the most individualist, none team oriented, action we can have in life. (The irony of "There is no 'I' in team!")

Integrity is a trait that seems to be evaporating over the past 200 years. In past time there was an honor code that instilled this mindset, to the point of a dueling. The reasoning behind this dueling seemed to be: if your honor or integrity was impugned it was better to be dead. It is debatable if eliminating the practice of dueling was a perfectly good thing, but, thank goodness it is no longer practiced.

Islamic countries where killing a family member who dishonors the family name is still practiced. This is the epitome of hypocrisy, defending one's honor by killing someone else or a family member, in order to demonstrate your integrity. This is a grave depravity. It difficult to grasp how this sort of thinking can infect an entire society, and be considered acceptable or even honorable.

But practically, the elimination of dueling was good and honor killing is a human tragedy. If a person is simply a better shot does not give him any more integrity. In contrast, if one does not have integrity and conducts his life in a hypocritical manner, it maybe better to be dead. The damage imparted on society because of this deficiency is far reaching and extremely contagious as it sets an example that is used as an excuse by future generations to do the similar bad things, without realizing the harm it brings.

# Acknowledgements

I want to take this page to mention and acknowledge those personalities I had the good fortune to meet and interact with, to spawn ideas I felt were insightful enough to write this book.

I must thank the late J. Paul McIntosh for his encouragement to pursue a second book after I shared the consternations of my first book. The encouragement was at his suggestion by saying that the "integrity issue" mentioned as a core value and necessary in any problem solving, should have been addressed before writing "The Grand Unification Theory of Business and Success". But the past is past and this book is the prequel.

I am also gratified for the interest shown by Lona Ferguson in my efforts along with her support and encouragement to continue pursuing this narrative. Her ability for noticing nuances and logic strings was helpful in completing concepts so they were more understandable and insightful.

I need to express my appreciation to Jeannie Ash for referring me to concepts, literature and her associations with famous authors who were studying and writing on similar concepts and topics.

I thank Don Cordes, Karen Walters and Dr. Ed Truemper for their insights on health care that helped me define our country's social contract and where it meets our personal contract with society.

I appreciate the dialogues with Jim Mallatt, Roland (Buzz) Nelson as well as Jeannie Ash for their diligence in vetting the premise of this book. They suffered through my explanations while encouraging me to "flesh out" incomplete thought processes to conclude the logic strings found in this book.

I need to mention Ellen Havlovic-Jirovsky's influence on the title of the book and by introducing me to Fr. Shawn Kilkawley. He works for the Dioceses of Lincoln, Nebraska, dealing with social and family issues. His seminars sparked conclusions that caused me to better understand the tendencies of our society and focus on symptoms and not the problem. This paradigm caused me to identify these limitations helping in more effective problem solving procedures.

I am grateful for the graphic design and production of the cover by Kim Sawatzke. It is his understanding of what I am trying to communicate that gives true mean to the saying "A picture is worth a thousand words".

I appreciate the listening ear and insightful wisdom of Brook Curtiss and Jim Mallatt in the content editing and production process of getting a book like this into reality. The need to explore the variations in the thought process is difficult, if not impossible, to do alone. Their input has made me more aware of and considerate of different points of view that can influence conclusions.

I want to thank my cartoonist, Neil Kay of Fiverr with the pseudo name "Adnielk" for his expertise and creative ability to literally make a picture worth a thousand words in communicating the ideas I was trying to express.

To all of you and those who had associations with me, during this process that had subliminal influences, I sincerely thank you.

Keith

# References

1. **Subsidiarity:** a principle of social doctrine that all social bodies exist for the sake of the individual so that what individuals are able to do, society should not take over, and what small societies can do, larger societies should not take over.

2. **Thomism:** the philosophical school that arose as a legacy of the work and thought of Thomas Aquinas (1225–1274), philosopher, theologian, and Doctor of the Church. In philosophy, his disputed questions and commentaries on Aristotle are perhaps his most well-known works. In theology, his Summa Theological is one of the most influential documents in medieval theology and continues to be the central point of reference for the philosophy and theology of the Catholic Church.

3. **ISIS:** The Islamic State of Iraq and the Levant (ISIL), also known as the Islamic State of Iraq and Syria (ISIS) Islamic State (IS), and by its Arabic language acronym Daesh is a Salafi jihadist unrecognized state and militant group that follows a fundamentalist, Wahhabi doctrine of Sunni Islam. Its adoption of the name Islamic State and its idea of a caliphate have been widely criticized, with the United Nations, various governments, and mainstream Muslim groups rejecting its statehood.

4. **Adolph Hitler:** 20 April 1889 – 30 April 1945) was a German politician who was the leader of the Nazi Party (Nationalsozialistische Deutsche Arbeiterpartei; NSDAP), Chancellor of Germany from 1933 to 1945, and Führer ("leader") of Nazi Germany from 1934 to 1945. As dictator of the German Reich, he initiated World War II in Europe with the invasion of Poland in September 1939 and was a central figure of the Holocaust.

5. **John Edwards:** Johnny Reid "John" Edwards (born June 10, 1953) is a former American politician, who served as a U.S. Senator from North Carolina. He was the Democratic nominee for Vice President in 2004, and was a candidate for the Democratic presidential nomination in 2004 and 2008.

6. **Titanic:** RMS Titanic was a British passenger liner that sank in the North Atlantic Ocean in the early morning of 15 April 1912, after colliding with an iceberg during her maiden voyage from Southampton to New York City. Of the 2,224 passengers and crew aboard, more than 1,500 died, making it one of the deadliest commercial peacetime maritime disasters in modern history. The largest ship afloat at the time it entered service, the RMS Titanic was the second of three Olympic class ocean liners operated by the White Star Line, and was built by the Harland and Wolff shipyard in Belfast. Thomas Andrews, her architect, died in the disaster.

7: **Pandora's Box:** is an artifact in Greek mythology, taken from the myth of Pandora's creation in Hesiod's Works and Days. The "box" was actually a large jar (given to Pandora "all-gifted, all-giving"), which contained all the evils of the world. Pandora opened the jar and all the evils flew out, leaving only "Hope" inside once she had closed it again. Today the phrase "to open Pandora's box" means to perform an action that may seem small or innocent, but that turns out to have severely detrimental and far-reaching negative consequences. The action cannot be reversed.

8: **David Hilbert:** 23 January 1862 – 14 February 1943) was a German mathematician. He is recognized as one of the most influential and universal mathematicians of the 19th and early 20th centuries. Hilbert discovered and developed a broad range of fundamental ideas in many areas, including invariant theory and the axiomatization of geometry. He also formulated the theory of Hilbert spaces, one of the foundations of functional analysis.

9. **Prayer of St. Francis:** The text most commonly called Prayer of Saint Francis, also known as the Peace Prayer or Make Me an Instrument of Your Peace, is a widely known Christian prayer. Often attributed to the 13th-century saint Francis of Assisi, the prayer in its present form cannot be traced back further than 1912, when it was printed in Paris in French, in a small spiritual magazine called La Clochette (The Little Bell), published by La Ligue de la Sainte-Messe (The League of the Holy Mass). The author's name was not given, although it may have been the founder of La Ligue, Fr. Esther Bouquerel.

10. **1984:** A dystopian novel by English author George Orwell published in 1949. The novel is set in Airstrip One (formerly known as Great Britain), a province of the superstate Oceania in a world of perpetual war, omnipresent government surveillance, and public manipulation, dictated by a political system euphemistically named English Socialism (or Ingsoc in the government's invented language, Newspeak) under the control of a privileged elite of the Inner Party, that persecutes individualism and independent thinking as "thought crime."

11. **Gilda Susan Radner:** (June 28, 1946 – May 20, 1989) was an American comedian, actress, and one of seven original cast members of the NBC sketch comedy show Saturday Night Live. In her routines, Radner specialized in broad and obnoxious parodies of television stereotypes such as annoying advice specialists and news anchors. She also portrayed those characters in her successful one-woman show on Broadway in 1979. After Radner was told her ovarian cancer had gone into remission, she wrote "It's Always Something" (a catchphrase of her character Roseanne Roseannadanna), which included details of her struggle with the illness.

12. **Murphy's Law:** is an adage or epigram that is typically stated as: Anything that can go wrong, will go wrong.

13. **Joe Paterno:** December 21, 1926 – January 22, 2012), sometimes referred to as "Joe Pa", was an American college football player, and later athletic director and coach. He was the head coach of the Penn State Nittany Lions from 1966 to 2011. With 409 victories, Paterno is the most victorious coach in NCAA FBS history. His illustrious career ended with his dismissal from the team in November, 2011 as a result of the Penn State child sex abuse scandal.

14. **Peyton Place:** is a 1956 novel by Grace Metalious. The novel describes how three women are forced to come to terms with their identity, both as women and as sexual beings, in a small, conservative, gossipy New England town, with recurring themes of hypocrisy, social inequities and class privilege in a tale that includes incest, abortion, adultery, lust and murder. It sold 60 000 copies within the first ten days of its release and remained on the New York Times best seller list for 59 weeks.

15. **Red Tape:** is an idiom that refers to excessive regulation or rigid conformity to formal rules that is considered redundant or bureaucratic and hinders or prevents action or decision-making. It is usually applied to governments, corporations, and other large organizations.

16. **Rotary:** is an international service organization whose stated purpose is to bring together business and professional leaders in order to provide humanitarian services, encourage high ethical standards in all vocations, and to advance goodwill and peace around the world. It is a secular organization open to all people regardless of race, color, creed, religion, gender, or political preference. There

are 34,282 member clubs worldwide. 1.2 million individuals called Rotarians have joined these clubs.

17. **Natural Law:** is a philosophy that certain rights or values are inherent by virtue of human nature and can be universally understood through human reason. Historically, natural law refers to the use of reason to analyze both social and personal human nature to deduce binding rules of moral behavior. The law of nature, as it is determined by nature, is universal.......

18. **O.J. Simpson:** Orenthal James "O. J." Simpson (born July 9, 1947), nicknamed The Juice, is a former American football running back, broadcaster, actor, and convicted felon. Simpson was acquitted of the 1994 murders of his ex-wife, Nicole Brown-Simpson and her friend, Ronald Goldman, after a lengthy and internationally publicized criminal trial, the *People v. Simpson.* In September 2007, Simpson was arrested in Las Vegas, Nevada, and charged with numerous felonies, including armed robbery and kidnapping. In 2008, he was convicted and sentenced to 33 years imprisonment, with a minimum of nine years without parole. He is serving his sentence at the Lovelock Correctional Center in Lovelock, Nevada.

19. **Alpha Type:** In studies of social animals, the highest ranking individual is sometimes designated as the alpha. Males, females, or both, can be alphas, depending on the species. Where one male and one female fulfill this role together, they are sometimes referred to as the alpha pair. Other animals in the same social group may exhibit deference or other species-specific subordinate behaviors towards the alpha or alphas.

20: **Beta Type:** Beta animals often act as second-in-command to the reigning alpha or alphas and will act as new alpha animals if an alpha dies or is otherwise no longer considered an alpha. In some species of birds, males pair up in twos when courting, the beta male aiding the alpha male. It has been found that the social context of the animals has a significant impact on courtship behavior and the overall reproductive success of that animal.

21. **Benjamin Franklin:** (January 17, 1706 – April 17, 1790) was one of the Founding Fathers of the United States. Franklin was a renowned polymath and a leading author, printer, political theorist, politician, freemason, postmaster, scientist, inventor, civic activist, statesman, and diplomat. As a scientist, he was a major figure in the American Enlightenment and the history of physics for his discoveries and theories regarding electricity. As an inventor, he is known for the lightning rod, bifocals, and the Franklin stove, among other inventions.[2] He facilitated many civic organizations, including Philadelphia's fire department and The University of Pennsylvania, an Ivy League institution.

22. **GMO:** A genetically modified organism (GMO) is any organism whose genetic material has been altered using genetic engineering techniques (i.e., a genetically *engineered* organism). GMOs are used to produce many medications and genetically modified foods and are widely used in scientific research and the production of other goods. The term GMO is very close to the technical legal term, 'living modified organism', defined in the Cartagena Protocol on Biosafety, which regulates international trade in living GMOs (specifically, "any living organism that possesses a novel combination of genetic material obtained through the use of modern biotechnology").

23. **Mason Jar:** A glass container named after American John Landis Mason who first invented and patented it in 1858, is a molded glass jar used in home canning to preserve food. The jar's mouth has a screw

thread on its outer perimeter to accept a metal ring (or "band").

24. **Parable of the Talents:** (also the **Parable of the Minas**), is one of the parables of Jesus, which appear in two of the synoptic, canonical gospels of the New Testament.

25. **GLBTQ:** is an initialism that stands for lesbian, gay, bisexual, transgender and queer or questioning. In use since the 1990s, the term is an adaptation of the initialism LGB, which was used to replace the term *gay* in reference to the LGBT community beginning in the mid-to-late 1980s. Activists believed that the term *gay community* did not accurately represent all those to whom it referred.

26. **Conservatism:** as a political and social philosophy promotes retaining traditional social institutions in the context of culture and civilization. Conservatives seek to preserve institutions like the Church, monarchy and the social hierarchy, as they are, emphasizing stability and continuity, while others, called reactionaries, oppose modernism and seek a return to "the way things were". The first established use of the term in a political context originated with François-René de Chateaubriand in 1818, during the period of Bourbon restoration that sought to roll back the policies of the French Revolution. The term, historically associated with right-wing politics, has since been used to describe a wide range of views.

27. **Liberalism:** is a political philosophy or worldview founded on ideas of liberty and equality. Whereas classical liberalism emphasizes the role of liberty, social liberalism stresses the importance of equality. Liberals espouse a wide array of views depending on their understanding of these principles, but generally they support ideas and programs such as freedom of speech, freedom of the press, freedom of religion, free markets, civil rights, democratic

societies, secular governments, gender equality, and international cooperation.

28. The **American Revolutionary War:** (1775–1783), also referred to as the **American War of Independence** and the **Revolutionary War** in the United States, was an armed conflict between Great Britain and thirteen of its North American colonies, which later declared its independence as the United States of America.

29. **Kenneth Wayne "Ken" Jennings III:** (born May 23, 1974) is an American game show contestant and author. Jennings holds the record for the longest winning streak on the U.S. syndicated game show *Jeopardy!* and as being the second highest-earning contestant in game show history.

30. **Bradford Gates "Brad" Rutter:** (born January 31, 1978) is the biggest all-time money winner on the U.S. syndicated game show *Jeopardy!* and the highest-earning American game show contestant of all time.

31. **The Crown:** is the state in all its aspects within the jurisprudence of the Commonwealth realms and their sub-divisions (such as Crown dependencies, provinces or states), although the term is not only a metonym for *the State*. The Crown is a corporation sole that represents the legal embodiment of executive, legislative, and judicial governance. It developed first in the Kingdom of England as a separation of the literal crown and property of the nation state from the person and personal property of the monarch.

32. **Greenhouse Gas:** (abbrev. **GHG**) is a gas in an atmosphere that absorbs and emits radiation within the thermal infrared range. This process is the fundamental cause of the greenhouse effect. The primary greenhouse gases in Earth's atmosphere are water vapor, carbon

dioxide, methane, nitrous oxide, and ozone. Without greenhouse gases, the average temperature of Earth's surface would be about −18 °C (0 °F), rather than the present average of 15 °C (59 °F). In the Solar System, the atmospheres of Venus, Mars and Titan also contain gases that cause a greenhouse effect.

33.   **EPA:** commonly refers to the United States Environmental Protection Agency.

34.   **Greenhouse gases:** are those gases that absorb and emit infrared radiation in the wavelength range emitted by Earth. In order, the most abundant greenhouse gases in Earth's atmosphere are: Water vapor (H2O), Carbon dioxide (CO2), Methane (CH4), Nitrous oxide (N2O), Ozone (O3), Chlorofluorocarbons (CFCs). Dust also contributes to the greenhouse gas affect that stabilizes the Earth's surface temperature.

35. **Albert Arnold "Al" Gore, Jr.:**   (born March 31, 1948) is an American politician and environmentalist who served as the 45th Vice President of the United States from 1993 to 2001 under President Bill Clinton. He was Clinton's running mate in their successful campaign in 1992, and was re-elected in 1996. At the end of Clinton's second term, Gore was picked as the Democratic nominee for the 2000 presidential election. After leaving office, Gore remained prominent as an author and environmental activist, whose work in climate change activism earned him (jointly with the IPCC) the Nobel Peace Prize in 2007.

36. **Carbon dioxide (CO$_2$):**  is an important trace gas in Earth's atmosphere currently constituting about 0.04%, i.e. 400 parts per million (ppm), of the atmosphere. Despite its relatively small concentration, CO$_2$ is a potent greenhouse gas and plays a vital role in regulating Earth's surface temperature through radioactive forcing and the greenhouse effect. Reconstructions show that

concentrations of $CO_2$ in the atmosphere have varied, ranging from as high as 7,000 ppm during the Cambrian period about 500 million years ago to as low as 180 ppm during the Quaternary glaciation of the last two million years.

37. **Big Bang Theory:** The Big Bang theory is an effort to explain what happened at the very beginning of our universe. Discoveries in astronomy and physics have shown beyond a reasonable doubt that our universe did in fact have a beginning. Prior to that moment there was nothing; during and after that moment there was something: our universe. The big bang theory is an effort to explain what happened during and after that moment.

38. The **Sacrament of Penance and Reconciliation:** (commonly called **Penance, Reconciliation,** or **Confession**) is one of the seven sacraments of the Catholic Church (called sacred mysteries in the Eastern Catholic Churches), in which the faithful obtain absolution for the sins committed against God and neighbor and are reconciled with the community of the Church. By this sacrament Christians are freed from sins committed after Baptism. The sacrament of Penance is considered the normal way to be absolved from mortal sin, by which one would otherwise condemn oneself to Hell.

39. **Disability Numbers:** About 56.7 million people, 19 percent of the population, had a disability in 2010, according to a broad definition of disability, with more than half of them reporting the disability was severe, according to a comprehensive report on this population released today by the U.S. Census Bureau.

40. **Cheaters in Welfare system:** According to the U.S. Department of Labor statistics website, based on the 2012 IPIA three-Year average data report, **fraud was prevalent in 2.67% of cases.** XML and XLS

Unemployment Insurance data sheets released yearly available at: U.S. Department of Labor

39. **Social Justice:** assigns rights and duties in the institutions of society, which enables people to receive the basic benefits and burdens of cooperation. The relevant institutions often include taxation, social insurance, public health, public school, public services, labor law and regulation of markets, to ensure fair distribution of wealth, and equal opportunity.

40. **Economic Freedom:** the ability of members of a society to undertake economic actions. This is a term used in economic and policy debates as well as in the philosophy of economics. One approach to economic freedom comes from classical liberal and libertarian traditions emphasizing free markets, free trade, and private property under free enterprise. Another approach to economic freedom extends the welfare economics study of individual choice, with greater economic freedom coming from a "larger" (in some technical sense) set of possible choices. Other conceptions of economic freedom include freedom from want and the freedom to engage in collective bargaining.

41. **Watson Computer:** is a question answering computer system capable of answering questions posed in natural language, developed in IBM's Deep QA project by a research team led by principal investigator David Ferrucci. Watson was named after IBM's first CEO, industrialist Thomas J. Watson. The computer system was specifically developed to answer questions on the quiz show Jeopardy! In 2011, Watson competed on Jeopardy, against former winners Brad Rutter and Ken Jennings. Watson received the first place prize of $1 million.

42. **Scarlet Letter:** an 1850 work of fiction in a historical setting, written by American author Nathaniel Hawthorne. The book is considered to be his "masterwork".

Set in 17th-century Puritan Massachusetts Bay Colony, during the years 1642 to 1649, it tells the story of Hester Prynne, who conceives a daughter through an affair and struggles to create a new life of repentance and dignity. Throughout the book, Hawthorne explores themes of legalism, sin, and guilt.

43. **Age of Enlightenment:** an intellectual movement which dominated the world of ideas in Europe during the 18th century, The Century of Philosophy. The Enlightenment included a range of ideas centered on reason as the primary source of authority and legitimacy, and came to advance ideals like liberty, progress, tolerance, fraternity, constitutional government, and separation of church and state.

44. **Survival of the fittest:** a phrase that originated from Darwinian evolutionary theory as a way of describing the mechanism of natural selection. The biological concept of fitness is defined as reproductive success. In Darwinian terms the phrase is best understood as "Survival of the form that will leave the most copies of itself in successive generations."

45. **Golden Rule:** principle of treating others as one would wish to be treated. It is a maxim of altruism seen in many human religions and human cultures. The maxim may appear as either a positive or negative injunction governing conduct:

46. **Klein Bottle:** an example of a non-orientable surface; it is a two-dimensional manifold against which a system for determining a normal vector cannot be consistently defined. Informally, it is a one-sided surface which, if traveled upon, could be followed back to the point of origin while flipping the traveler upside down. Other related non-orientable objects include the Möbius strip and the real projective plane. Whereas a Möbius strip is a

surface with boundary, a Klein bottle has no boundary (for comparison, a sphere is an orientable surface with no boundary).

47. **Mobius Strip:** surface with only one side and only one boundary. The Möbius strip has the mathematical property of being non-orientable. It can be realized as a ruled surface. It was discovered independently by the German mathematicians August Ferdinand Möbius and Johann Benedict Listing in 1858.

48. **Transgender/Bi-Sexual/Gay Percentage:** the NHIS reported in July 2014 that 1.6 percent of Americans identify as gay or lesbian, and 0.7 percent identify as bisexual. In a 'Williams Institute' review based on a June–September 2012 Gallup poll, approximately 3.4 percent of American adults identify themselves as being LGBT (lesbian, gay, bisexual, or transgender).

49. **Participation trophy:** Trophies for all convey an inaccurate and potentially dangerous life message to children: We are all winners. This message is repeated at the end of each sports season, year after year, and is only reinforced by the collection of trophies that continues to pile up. We begin to expect awards and praise for just showing up — to class, practice, after-school jobs — leaving us woefully unprepared for reality.

50. **Neville Chamberlin:** a British Conservative politician who served as Prime Minister of the United Kingdom from May 1937 to May 1940. Chamberlain is best known for his appeasement foreign policy, and in particular for his signing of the Munich Agreement in 1938, conceding the German-speaking Sudetenland region of Czechoslovakia to Germany. However, when Adolf Hitler later invaded Poland, the UK declared war on Germany on 3 September 1939, and Chamberlain led Britain through the first eight months of World War II.

51. **Social Contract:** a theory or model, originating during the Age of Enlightenment, that typically addresses the questions of the origin of society and the legitimacy of the authority of the state over the individual. Social contract arguments typically posit that individuals have consented, either explicitly or tacitly, to surrender some of their freedoms and submit to the authority of the ruler or magistrate (or to the decision of a majority), in exchange for protection of their remaining rights. The question of the relation between natural and legal rights, therefore, is often an aspect of social contract theory.

52. **Personal Contract:** The phrase used to describe that moral agreement that we, as human beings, have to our follow man in the way they are viewed, treated or described. It is another way of describing the "Golden Rule" (45)

53. **Milton Freidman:** an American economist who received the 1976 Nobel Memorial Prize in Economic Sciences for his research on consumption analysis, monetary history and theory, and the complexity of stabilization policy.

54. **Saul Alinsky:** (January 30, 1909 – June 12, 1972) was an American community organizer and writer. He is generally considered to be the founder of modern community organizing. He is often noted for his 1971 book Rules for Radicals.

55. **Rules for Radicals:** book published in 1971 by activist and writer Saul D. Alinsky shortly before his death. His goal for the Rules for Radicals was to create a guide for future community organizers to use in uniting low-income communities, or "Have-Nots", in order for them to gain social, political, legal, and economic power. Within it, Alinsky compiled the lessons he had learned throughout his experiences of community organizing from 1939–1971 and

targeted these lessons at the current, new generation of radicals.

56. **Federalism:** the mixed or compound mode of government, combining a general government (the central or 'federal' government) with regional governments (provincial, state, cantonal, territorial or other sub-unit governments) in a single political system.

57. **Torah:** the central reference of Judaism. It has a range of meanings. It can most specifically mean the first five books (Pentateuch) of the twenty-four books of the Tanakh, and it usually includes the rabbinic commentaries

58. **Quran:** literally meaning "the recitation"; also Romanized **Qur'an** or **Koran**) is the central religious text of Islam, which Muslims believe

**59. Buddhism:** is a religion and dharma that encompasses a variety of traditions, beliefs and spiritual practices largely based on teachings attributed to the Buddha.

**60. Hinduism:** is a religion, or a way of life, found most notably in India and Nepal. Hinduism has been called the oldest religion in the world, and some practitioners and scholars refer to it as Sanātana Dharma, "the eternal law," or the "eternal way,

**61. Good Samaritan:** A parable about a traveler who is stripped of clothing, beaten, and left half dead alongside the road. First a priest and then a Levite comes by, but both avoid the man. Finally, a Samaritan happens upon the traveler. Samaritans and Jews generally despised each other, but the Samaritan helps the injured man.

**62. British Thermal Units (BTU):** is a traditional unit of heat; it is defined as the amount of heat required to raise the temperature of one pound of water by one degree Fahrenheit. It is part of the British Imperial system of units.

63. **Sharyl Attkisson:** American author and host of the weekly Sunday public affairs program 'Full Measure with Sharyl Attkisson' which airs on television stations operated by the Sinclair Broadcasting Group.

64. **TED:** (Technology, Entertainment, Design) is an invitation only event where world's leading thinkers and doers gather to hear presentations of current topics with unique perspective that are not readily apparent or of common knowledge.

65: **Wikipedia:** A free online encyclopedia, created and edited by volunteers around the world and hosted by the Wikimedia Foundation.

66: **Astroturfing:** an analogy for the concept where information or an issue appears to be originating from a common consensus of a majority of the people, but in fact from a small special interest group. A term used to contrast the analogy of 'grass roots' or an honest movement with a fabricated movement.

67: **Bots:** A computer algorithm that runs the gamut from generating massive reposting of fake news to unjustly sway public opinion, to blasting websites on the internet causing the denial of service for legitimist businesses.

68: **Modernity:** a term used in the humanities and social sciences to designate both a historical period (the modern era), as well as the ensemble of particular socio-cultural norms, attitudes and practices that arose in post-medieval Europe and have developed since, in various ways and at various times, around the world. While it includes a wide range of interrelated historical processes and cultural phenomena (from fashion to modern warfare), it can also refer to the subjective or existential experience of the conditions they produce, and their ongoing impact on human culture, institutions, and politics

**69. Paul Shanklin**: an American conservative political satirist, impressionist, comedian, and conservative speaker. Shanklin writes and voices the characters for, the songs and satirical comedy segments used by conservative radio host Rush Limbaugh.

**70. The Cloud:** a type of Internet-based computing that provides shared computer processing resources and data to computers and other devices on demand. It is a model for enabling ubiquitous, on-demand access to a shared pool of configurable computing resources (e.g., computer networks, servers, storage, applications and services), which can be rapidly provisioned and released with minimal management effort.

**71. PBS:** an American non-profit public broadcaster and television program distributor headquartered in Arlington, Virginia. PBS is an independently operated nonprofit organization and is the most prominent provider of television programming to public television stations in the United States, distributing series such as Keeping Up Appearances, BBC World News, NOVA science NOW, NOVA, Barney and Friends, Arthur, Sesame Street, PBS News Hour, Walking with Dinosaurs, Masterpiece, Nature, American Masters, Frontline, and Antiques Roadshow.

**72. Synapse:** a structure that permits a neuron (or nerve cell) to pass an electrical or chemical signal to another neuron. Some authors generalize this concept to include the communication from a neuron to any other cell type, such as to a motor cell, although such non-neuronal contacts may be referred to as junctions (a historically older term).

**73. Capitalism:** an economic system based on private ownership of the means of production and their operation for profit.

**74. Imperialism:** an action that involves a country (usually an empire or kingdom) extending its power by the acquisition of territories. It may also include the exploitation of these territories, an action that is linked to colonialism. Colonialism is generally regarded as an expression of imperialism.

**75. Mercantilism:** an economic theory and practice that was dominant in Western Europe during the 15th to the mid-18th centuries. Mercantilism is a form of economic nationalism. Its goal is to enrich and empower the nation and state to the maximum degree, by acquiring and retaining as much economic activity as possible within the nation's borders.

**76. Socialism:** economic and social systems characterized by social ownership and democratic control of the means of production;[10] as well as the political ideologies, theories, and movements that aim to establish them.

**77. Problem Solving Method: (PSM)** a mathematical approach of solving problems by objectifying all parameters of consideration that are expected to be addressed in the solution. When the problem is perfectly defines in this manner with all agendas objectively quantified and the form of the solution envisioned, there is only one possible answer.

**78. Tough Love:** an expression used when someone treats another person harshly or sternly with the intent to help them in the long run.

**79. BART: Bay Area Rapid Transit** is a public transportation metro system serving the San Francisco Bay Area in California. The rapid transit elevated and subway system connects San Francisco with cities in Alameda, Contra Costa, and San Mateo counties. BART operates 5 routes on 104 miles (167 km) of track connecting 45 stations, plus a 3.2-mile (5.1 km) automated guideway transit line to the Oakland International Airport which adds an additional station.

**80. NAFTA:** The **North American Free Trade Agreement** is an agreement signed by Canada, Mexico, and the United States, creating a trilateral trade bloc in North America. The agreement came into force on January 1, 1994. It superseded the Canada–United States Free Trade Agreement between the U.S. and Canada.

**81. TPP:** The **Trans-Pacific Partnership** or the **Trans Pacific Partnership Agreement** (**TPPA**), is a trade agreement between Australia, Brunei, Canada, Chile, Japan, Malaysia, Mexico, New Zealand, Peru, Singapore, the United States (until 23 January 2017) and Vietnam.

**82. Schumk:** in American English is a pejorative term meaning one who is stupid or foolish, or an obnoxious, contemptible or detestable person. The word came into the English language from Yiddish (שמאָק, shmok), where it has similar pejorative meanings, but where its original and literal meaning is

**83. Democracy:** literally means "rule of the commoners", and is a system of government in which the citizens exercise power directly or elect representatives from among themselves to form a governing body, such as a parliament. Democracy is sometimes referred to as "rule of the majority".

**84. Republic:** a form of government in which the country is considered a "public matter", not the private concern or property of the rulers and where offices of state are elected or appointed, rather than inherited. It is a government where the head of state is not a monarch. In American English, the definition of a republic can also refer specifically to a government in which elected individuals represent the citizen body, known elsewhere as a representative democracy (a democratic republic),[4] and exercise power according to the rule of law (a constitutional republic)

**85. PETA:** People for the Ethical Treatment of Animals **PETA** is the largest animal rights organization in the world, with more than 3 million members in the United States

**86. Versailles Treaty:** was the most important of the peace treaties that brought World War I to an end. The Treaty ended the state of war between Germany and the Allied Powers. It was signed on 28 June 1919, exactly five years after the assassination of Archduke Franz Ferdinand. The other Central Powers on the German side of World War I signed separate treaties.[8] Although the armistice, signed on 11 November 1918, ended the actual fighting, it took six months of Allied negotiations at the Paris Peace Conference to conclude the peace treaty. The treaty was registered by the Secretariat of the League of Nations on 21 October 1919.

**87. Rubbernecking:** is the act of staring at something of interest. The term *rubbernecking* refers to the physical act of craning one's neck, performed in order to get a better view. Rubberneck has been described as a human trait that is associated with morbid curiosity. In the times of telephone party lines, it was the name use to describe an individual who was secretly listening to phone conversations of other parties using the telephone line.

**88. Car Talk:** a Peabody Award-winning radio talk show broadcast weekly on NPR stations and elsewhere. Its subjects were automobiles and automotive repair, discussed often in a humorous way. It was hosted by Brothers Tom and Ray Magliozzi, known also as "Click and Clack, the Tappet Brothers".

**89. Electoral College:** the mechanism established by the United States Constitution for the indirect election of the President of the United States and Vice President of the United States. Citizens of the United States vote in each state at a general election to choose a slate of "electors" pledged to vote for a party's candidate.

**90. Term Limits:** apply to many offices at both the federal and state level, and date back to the American Revolution. Term limits, also referred to as *rotation in office*, restrict the number of terms of office an officeholder may hold.

**91. Entropy:** is conserved for a reversible process. A reversible process is one that does not deviate from thermodynamic equilibrium, while producing the maximum work. Any process which happens quickly enough to deviate from thermal equilibrium cannot be reversible. In these cases energy is lost to heat, total entropy increases, and the potential for maximum work to be done in the transition is also lost. More specifically, total entropy is conserved in a reversible process and not conserved in an irreversible process.

**92. OSHA:** The **Occupational Safety and Health Administration** is an agency of the United States Department of Labor. Congress established the agency under the Occupational Safety and Health Act, which

President Richard M. Nixon signed into law on December 29, 1970. OSHA's mission is to "assure safe and healthful working conditions for working men and women by setting and enforcing standards and by providing training, outreach, education and assistance".

**93. Single Payer Health Care System:** is a healthcare system in which the state, financed by taxes, covers basic healthcare costs for all residents regardless of income, occupation, or health status. The alternatives include "multi-payer" systems in which private individuals or their employers buy health insurance or healthcare services from private or public providers.

**94. Alexander the Great: Alexander III of Macedon** (20/21 July 356 BC – 10/11 June 323 BC) was a king of the Ancient Greek kingdom of Macedon and a member of the Argead dynasty. He was born in Pella in 356 BC and succeeded his father Philip II to the throne at the age of twenty.

**95. Asperger's Syndrom:** also known as **Asperger's**, is a developmental disorder characterized by significant difficulties in social interaction and nonverbal communication, along with restricted and repetitive patterns of behavior and interests.

# Index

1984 ................................................... 54, 223

Abortion ............................ 112, 135, 157, 224

Addictions ........................................ 113, 178

Adolph Hitler ........ 22, 28, 48, 62, 188, 216, 221

Age of Enlightenment ................... 134, 232, 234

Albert Gore ....................................... 148, 229

Alexander the Great ............................. 77, 78

Alpha Type ........................................ 34, 225

American Revolution ................................ 228

Asperger's Syndrome .......................... 128, 242

Astroturfing ............................ 165, 195, 236

Balance of Trade ........................................ 70

Bay Area Rapid Transit (BART) .............. 62, 239

Ben Franklin ............................................ 186

Beta Type ......................................... 34, 226

Big Bang Theory ................................ 158, 230

Bible .......................................... 92, 127, 177

| | |
|---|---|
| **Brad Rutter** | 125, 232 |
| **Buddhism** | 127, 235 |
| **Car Talk** | 56, 241 |
| **Capitalism** | 49, 158, 238 |
| **Conservatism** | 227 |
| **David Hilbert** | 11, 57, 222 |
| **Decision Tree** | 125 |
| **Democratic Republic** | 69, 129, 188, 240 |
| **Donald Trump** | 24, 44, 194 |
| **Electoral College** | 135, 241 |
| **Entropy** | 207, 209, 241 |
| **Environmental Protection Agency** | 145, 229 |
| **European Union** | 77, 79 |
| **Euthanasia** | 112 |
| **Federalism** | 91, 235 |
| **Gilda S. Radner** | 108, 223 |
| **GMO** | 106, 109, 157, 226 |
| **Golden Rule** | 181, 201, 232 |

**Good Samaritan** ............................. 236, 244

**Greece** .............................................. 77, 80

**Hinduism** ...................................... 127, 235

**Imperialism** .................................... 49, 238

**ISIS** ............................... 17, 47, 62, 221

**Job Creation** ....................................... 85

**Joe Paterno** .................................. 30, 224

**John Edwards** .............................. 222, 245

**Judicial Activism** ............................... 137

**Ken Jennings** ............................... 125, 232

**Klein Bottle** .................................. 215, 233

**Laws of Economics** ........................... 245

**Liberalism** ......................................... 228

**Mason Jar** .................................. 109, 227

**Mercantilism** ................................ 49, 238

**Milton Freidman** ........................... 43, 234

**Mobius Strip** ............................... 215, 233

**Modernity** ............................ 21, 211, 237

Murphy's Law ............................................. 83, 224

Natural Law ...... 11, 37, 119, 138, 176, 202, 225

Neville Chamberlin ......................................... 234

No. Amer. Free Trade (NAFTA) ............... 72, 239

O.J. Simpson ............................................ 30, 225

PBS ...................................................... 197, 237

Pandora's Box ............................................... 222

Parable of the Talents .......................... 227, 236

Participation Trophy ............................ 22, 233

Paul Shanklin ........................................ 168, 237

Peyton Place ............................................ 30, 224

PETA .............................................. 106, 109, 240

Personal Contract ............. 89, 91, 103, 214, 234

Political Correctness. 14, 64, 146, 168, 181, 206

Prayer of St. Francis ............................... 48, 223

Problem Solving Method ............. 3, 24, 123, 239

Quran ................................................... 127, 235

Rubbernecking ........................................ 30, 241

Red Tape ........................ 123, 190, 224

Republic ................... 65, 119, 124, 178, 230

Robin Hood ............................................ 69

Rotary ..................................... 202, 224

Sacrament of Penance ...................... 210, 230

Scarlet Letter ................................ 13, 232

Schmuck ........................................ 77, 112

Sin of Omission ................. 86, 102, 162, 171

Single Payer Health Care ..................... 115, 259

Social Contract ........... 67, 73, 89, 103, 219, 234

Socialism ............... 49, 157, 167, 186, 223, 238

Subsidiarity ................................... X, 221

Survival of the Fittest ..... 33, 158, 173, 232, 249

Synapse ..................................... 197, 238

Tariffs ..................................... 66, 71

Ten Commandments ............... 38, 127, 138, 202

Term Limits ................................ 136, 241

The Cloud ................................... 189, 227

The Crown ............................................. 134, 228

Thomistic ......................................................... 2

Titanic ..................................................... 23, 222

Trans-Pacific Trade Agreement ............... 65, 239

Tough Love ........................... 105, 239, 249, 254

Tort Reform ................................................... 139

Torah ................................................... 127, 235

TPP ........................................................ 72, 239

Utopian World ................................................. 89

Versailles Treaty ............................ 12, 23, 240

Watson Computer ............. X, 125, 142, 197, 248

We die as we live ......................................... 248

Welfare ........................... 85, 89, 231, 249, 254

# The Solution to all the World's Problems

Every societal or political problem is caused by competing agendas that arise from violating this most important core value, "integrity". It is difficult to exactly define it with an explanation; "It is like pornography, I know it when I see It." might be a close approximation.

Integrity is that aura of being exactly as one appears. The Mobus Strip on the cover is a near perfect analogy......it demonstrates a trait where it is impossible to know the difference between the inside and the outside. The same this is true with integrity. Your deepest thoughts are no different than your actions the world sees.

We live in a world where the word "social justice" [is] a tool to advance an agenda that can not be advanced without "victims". The mere use of the words social justice automatically implies the existence of a victim class and the movement always accuses the opposition as being coldhearted and cruel, when tough love is tried. The victimization of someone is not possible if true integrity was present.

The words "economic freedom" requires the concept of self reliance and is the near perfect antonym for social justice. Once a victim is created, that victim will always have a reason for failure. This is the social infection of the welfare system and is self perpetuating. This is caused by a fundamental lack of integrity. Allowing oneself to become a victim is not a natural occurrence because it is contrary to our "survival of the fittest" tendency. This dependency is learned from the previous generations of welfare recipients and is a result of a lack of integrity, by allowing dependency to continue.

Governments typically use macro approaches in their attempt at solving problems. They always look for the silver bullet or a "one size fits all" solution that typically addresses only the symptom. This happens because it is the easiest and the simplest approach and is always tried first. They always wrongly address the symptom because if they solved the problem, they would be out of a job. This is another example where integrity is lacking.

The government might say they want easy solutions, but they are lying. It seems when any solution is considered, if it is too simple or easy and it is overlooked because of the numerous other alternatives they feel should also be considered because of their concept of "democracy". Their belief is everyone should have a voice and have some input. This is a flawed problem solving technique. It results in having no concept of what a reasonable solution looks like and no one wants to take responsibility if it doesn't work. It also allows blame to be place on their constitutes by claiming "that is what they wanted" as their excuse. This requires "perfecting the question", a process where true integrity is applied giving the answer to all the world's problems and not the symptom. The mantra: "I would rather be respected than liked." is an indication of true integrity.

The pain we experience with our government, trying to fix problems, is due to a lack of integrity.....we can't seem to trust them. Their continuing the analysis of the symptom is a delaying process. It used as an excuse for not fixing anything, and a delaying tactic for getting nothing done. Their use of this flawed process, often considered a badge of courage, broadcasting "how hard" they are working on the issue, is used as a selling point and simply a lie.
This book will show how to identify the problem, and not the symptom, with a method of "perfecting the question" that will give the answers to all the world's problems.

# List of Universal Truths and Unequivocals

1. No one likes a know-it-all
2. Everybody goes to the bathroom
3. Nobody is always right
4. The truth in any story is always in the middle
5. People care only about what interests them
6. We all have exactly the same amount of time every day
7. We won't get out of here alive
8. People change only when they can't tolerate where they are
9. Everyone enjoys being entertained or amused
10. We all want to be liked
11. Nobody has enough money
12. Money won't make you happy
13. One can not give enough
14. Sex is how we all got here
15. Only Christ was perfectly altruistic
16. Denial is easiest recognized in someone else
17. Everyone has a one thing where they are above average
18. You always find everything in the last place you look
19. Jobs only exist to solve the problem of someone else
20. Interested is interesting
21. Everyone snores!

And one that I'm still working on: "Women are always right !"

# About the Author

Keith was born on North coast of Nebraska with his formative years spent on a farm/ranch operation. That experience taught the true meaning of integrity and being self sufficient. His understanding of what a true Renaissance Man is came through the example of his grandfather, Frank, who lived on the farming operation with his father Norman.

Their encouragement to reason, question, conclude and implement the actions necessary to survive, was the basis for forming many of his conclusions expressed in this book.

Their objective was simple: keep the farm/ranch operation going and it still remains in the family after 5 generations.

His objective for this book: do what ever is necessary to make the world a better place.

Upon graduating from the University of Nebraska as a civil engineer, he worked as a Petrochemical process Engineer, Real Estate broker, Investment Banker, Management Consultant, Politician and now an author.

Contact his web site www.keithkube.com for information on arranging speaking engagements for service organizations or schools.

Made in the USA
Coppell, TX
25 August 2021